A Sincere *and* Pure Devotion *to* Christ

100 DAILY MEDITATIONS
on 2 CORINTHIANS

Volume I
2 Corinthians 1–6

SAM STORMS

WHEATON, ILLINOIS

Two Volume Set ISBN: 978-1-4335-1311-4

Volume 1
Trade Paperback ISBN: 978-1-4335-1150-9
PDF ISBN: 978-1-4335-1151-6
Mobipocket ISBN: 978-1-4335-1152-3
ePub ISBN: 978-1-4335-2382-3

Volume 2
Trade Paperback ISBN: 978-1-4335-1308-4
PDF ISBN: 978-1-4335-1309-1
Mobipocket ISBN: 978-1-4335-1310-7
ePub ISBN: 978-1-4335-2252-9

Library of Congress Cataloging-in-Publication Data
Storms, C. Samuel, 1951–
        A sincere and pure devotion to Christ : 100 daily meditations on 2 Corinthians / Sam Storms.
                p. cm.
        Includes bibliographical references.
        ISBN 978-1-4335-1150-9 (v. 1, tpb)—ISBN 978-1-4335-1308-4 (v. 2, tpb) 1. Bible. N.T. Corinthians, 2nd—Devotional literature. I. Title.

BS2675.54.S76 2010
242'.5—dc22   2009027808

Crossway is a publishing ministry of Good News Publishers.

To Melanie
my beloved daughter
A woman who has encountered God and persevered in faith
for the future he has promised her.

"For I know the plans I have for you, declares the LORD,
plans for welfare and not for evil, to give you a future and a hope."
(Jer. 29:11)

Contents

A Witness to Christ and a Window into the Heart of Paul

S aul of Tarsus, that energetic and highly educated Pharisee who took the name Paul following his saving encounter with the risen Christ on the road to Damascus, has become synonymous with Christianity. Some even contend that he, not Jesus, was its founder. Paul himself would have cringed at any such notion.

But who was this man? What made him tick? Why did he make the painful choices we read about in the New Testament? People who have tracked his missionary journeys and struggled to comprehend his many letters long to get inside his head and peer into his heart. What were his motives? How did he persevere in the face of unending hardship and excruciating persecution? What accounts for his unyielding commitment to Christ and his love for the many churches he established? What empowered him to endure the slander of those he served and to sacrifice himself for people who repaid his devotion with disdain and contempt?

One might think such experiences would compel Paul to withdraw within himself, to retreat relationally, to close off his heart and take whatever steps necessary to guard his wounded soul from further damage. I thank God daily that such never occurred. In fact, 2 Corinthians is a vivid portrayal of the courage, honesty, and vulnerability of this remarkable man. Unlike any of his other letters, in 2 Corinthians we hear his heart beat, we feel his passions, we are put in touch with his deepest fears and longings and loves.

It's not easy to move beyond the public image that people project to see into their very souls. Their true thoughts, intentions, motivations, anxieties, desires, greatest joys, and greatest disappointments are often hidden from sight, obscured beneath the complexities of human personality and relational defense mechanisms. If you've read much of the New Testament, you've no doubt wondered about such things in Paul. Unfortunately, you won't learn much about him from reading Romans or Galatians, his most theological writings. There's more to learn of him as a person in his two letters to Timothy, which were most likely written within months of Paul's martyrdom in Rome. But nowhere does Paul pull back the curtain on his life and expose his inner self to such a degree and with such brutal honesty as he does in 2 Corinthians.

If you've never studied this book before, you're in for a treat and a challenge. But don't think for a moment that this letter to the church in Corinth is primarily about Paul, or even the Corinthians themselves. It's about Jesus. Paul summed it up perfectly in chapter 4, verse 5: "For what we proclaim is not ourselves, but Jesus Christ as Lord, with ourselves as your servants for Jesus' sake." There it is. Jesus alone and always is Lord. He is supreme, central, and all-satisfying. He is the center and circumference of the gospel we proclaim. And we, Paul says, are here simply to proclaim that truth and serve you in such a way that you find in him complete joy and satisfaction for your souls, for his eternal glory. That is 2 Corinthians. I hope you enjoy the journey into this remarkable book and, through what you read, into the heart of a man whose life-long passion was to make known the glories of Christ Jesus for the joy of the church.

Coming to Corinth

In the summer of 1991 I was given the incredible opportunity of participating in a trip that traced Paul's missionary journeys. Athens, Thessalonica, Ephesus, and eventually Rome were included in our tour. So, too, was Corinth. As I stood among the ruins of that ancient city, I couldn't help but think about its storied history and the critical role it played in the early years of the Christian church.

The history of ancient Corinth is the story of two cities. Perhaps the first event of importance occurred in 146 BC, when a Roman army invaded and destroyed the city and killed or enslaved virtually the entire population. Corinth lay in ruins for more than a century, until 44 BC when Julius Caesar saw its great potential and gave orders that it be rebuilt as a Roman colony.

Not only did Corinth soon prosper because of its position as a port city, it also became one of Rome's most notable centers for banking and finance. We should also note its political significance. In 27 BC it became the seat of the region's proconsul and the capital of the senatorial province of Achaia until AD 15, when it became an imperial province. Corinth was also widely known for its hosting of the Isthmian games, a biennial athletic competition second only to the Olympic games in importance. Corinth soon was regarded as the third most important city of the empire after Rome and Alexandria.[1]

The Character of Corinth

First-century Corinth, with a population estimated to be as high as two hundred thousand, has been described as "a wide-open boomtown" comparable to San Francisco of the Gold Rush days. Corinth boasted two harbors and was strategically located, thus enhancing its reputation as one of the leading commercial centers of southern Greece. Sailors and merchants from every city and province, and therefore from every race and religion, passed through Corinth. It was truly cosmopolitan in nature.

Not unexpectedly, Corinth became notorious for luxurious and debauched living. Although virtually every pagan deity had a cult following in Corinth (archaeologists have discovered temples devoted to Neptune, Apollo, Venus, Octavia, Asclepius, Demeter, Core, and

Poseidon, among others), its chief shrine was the temple of Aphrodite (the Greek goddess of love and life), where as many as one thousand temple prostitutes were reported to have conducted their business. Sexual perversion and immorality of every conceivable (and some inconceivable) sort was rampant. One is not surprised, then, that the word "corinthianize" could mean to "fornicate" and was likely coined to refer to the opulence and pervasive vice for which this ancient city was known.

Corinth's reputation is notorious. Among other things, archaeologists have discovered there clay representations of human genitals that were offered to Asclepius, the god of healing. Evidently, the hope was that that part of the body, suffering from venereal disease, would be healed. However, it is important to point out that Corinth's reputation comes from what we know it to have been like prior to its devastation in 146 BC. Thus we should be careful "not to read the old city's character into the new city. . . . [Nevertheless], traditions like that die hard, and as a great port city it is unlikely that new Corinth established a reputation for moral probity (see 1 Cor. 6:12ff.)."[2]

Perhaps, then, we would be justified in comparing Corinth not only with the San Francisco of the Gold Rush days but with the San Francisco of today as well!

It was, however, in just such a place that the grace of God appeared. For here Paul spent a year and a half preaching the gospel.

The church in Corinth was composed largely of Gentiles, the majority of whom were at the lower end of the socio-economic ladder (although there were a few wealthy families). As Gordon Fee has noted, "although they were the Christian church in Corinth, an inordinate amount of Corinth was yet in them, emerging in a number of attitudes and behaviors that required radical surgery without killing the patient."[3] Both of Paul's canonical letters to this group of believers attempt to do this.

The Church in Corinth and Its Relationship to Paul

Paul's relationship to the Corinthians was a long and tempestuous one. From several statements in both his first and second epistles to the church, we are able to reconstruct a sequence of events.[4]

1. Paul first preaches the gospel in Corinth during his second missionary journey, probably in late AD 50 or early AD 51. He worked with Priscilla and Aquila as a tentmaker and probably lived with them. The results of Paul's initial ministry in Corinth are recorded in Acts 18:1–11. While there he regularly went to the synagogue and reasoned with both Jews and God-fearing Greeks, seeking to demonstrate, as was his custom, that Jesus was indeed the Messiah prophesied by the Old Testament Scriptures.

2. After one and a half years of ministry in Corinth, in the spring of AD 52, Paul made his way with Priscilla and Aquila to the city of Ephesus. After only a brief stay, he left them there and departed for Jerusalem. From there he went to Antioch, eventually returning to Ephesus where he remained for the next two and a half years (from the fall of AD 52 to the spring of AD 55). It was during this two-and-a-half-year period of ministry in Ephesus that Paul composed his Corinthian correspondence.

3. Sometime in late AD 54 Paul wrote a letter to the Corinthians that is now lost (see 1 Cor. 5:9–11). We will call this "Corinthian Letter A." He wrote this letter in response to news (either by personal report or a letter from the Corinthians) that some in Corinth had failed to separate from people within the church who had engaged in repeated sexual immorality. Evidently the Corinthians misinterpreted Paul, thinking that he was recommending they separate entirely from the wider Corinthian society.

4. Subsequent to this, Paul received reports from certain people in Chloe's house (1 Cor. 1:11) that there were problems in the Corinthian church, in particular the breaking up of the believing community into factions. Also, according to 1 Corinthians 16:17, three men (Stephanus, Fortunatus, and Achaicus) from Corinth came to him, evidently with a letter from the church asking Paul numerous questions about Christian behavior and belief (see 1 Cor. 7:1). In response to the report from Chloe's house and the questions asked of him, Paul wrote what we know as 1 Corinthians. We will call this "Corinthian Letter B" (probably written in late AD 54).

5. In "Corinthian Letter B" (our canonical 1 Corinthians), Paul revealed his travel plans. He hoped first to go to Macedonia and then make his way south to Corinth. However, after sending Timothy to

Corinth bearing the letter, he changed his plans slightly. Now he proposed to visit Corinth twice: first on his way to Macedonia and second on his way back from Macedonia (see 2 Cor. 1:15–16).

6. All of this changed yet again, however, when Timothy arrived in Corinth and discovered how bad the situation was. Timothy, or perhaps someone else, informed Paul of the distressing circumstances in Corinth and how the church had not responded to his letter (our 1 Corinthians).

7. Paul immediately put aside everything else and made an urgent visit to Corinth to try to put things right (probably in the spring of AD 55). This direct confrontation with the Corinthians turned out to be a bitter and humiliating experience for the apostle. He refers to it in 2 Corinthians 2:1 as a "painful visit" or one that caused "sorrow." Apparently the Corinthians not only ignored the instruction of 1 Corinthians (i.e., "Corinthian Letter B"), but also had given their allegiance to one or two men who opposed Paul, treated him with disrespect, and ridiculed his apostleship. Paul was deeply hurt and offended (see 2 Cor. 2:5–8, 10; 7:12).

8. Because of this distressing experience, Paul did not stay long in Corinth. He returned to Ephesus and determined not to make another painful visit to Corinth. Therefore, he called off the double stop he had earlier planned to make on his way to and from Macedonia (see 2 Cor. 1:15–16). All this did was to give his enemies an excuse to charge him with being fickle, a man who vacillated and really cared very little for the Corinthian believers and their feelings (2 Cor. 1:17).

9. Paul obviously could not leave matters unsettled. He feared that his enemies would destroy the work of the gospel in Corinth. Therefore, he wrote yet another letter to them (in the summer of AD 55). This one he describes as the "severe" or "tearful" letter (see 2 Cor. 2:4, 9). We will call it "Corinthian Letter C." In this letter he harshly rebuked the Corinthians and demanded the punishment of the man who had opposed and ridiculed him so maliciously (see 2 Cor. 2:3–4, 6, 9; 7:8–12). Titus was given the unenviable responsibility of carrying this letter to Corinth. Like "Corinthian Letter A," this piece of correspondence is also lost.

10. Paul remained in Ephesus, where he faced some of the worst opposition to the gospel he had yet encountered. He refers to this in 2 Corinthians 1:8–10. In late AD 55 he left Ephesus and went to Troas, hoping to meet Titus there with news of how the Corinthians had responded to the "severe/tearful" letter. Much to his chagrin, Titus was not there (see 2 Cor. 2:13). Evidently he and Titus had planned to meet in Macedonia should the meeting in Troas not occur. Hence, Paul made his way to Macedonia, anxiously awaiting the arrival of Titus from Corinth. While in Macedonia he ministered to the churches there and began collecting money to send to the Christians in Jerusalem who were suffering from famine (see 2 Cor. 8:1–2). Titus finally arrived from Corinth with the good news for which Paul had prayed (the apostle's response is described in 2 Cor. 7:5ff.). However, not all the news from Corinth was encouraging:

- Some had become critical of Paul for what they perceived to be vacillation in his travel plans; as far as they were concerned, this proved him to be a fleshly or carnal man who made self-serving decisions according to earthly standards of conduct (2 Cor. 1:12, 17).
- The collection begun by Titus for the church in Jerusalem had stalled (8:6, 10; 9:2).
- Despite what he had written in 1 Corinthians, some in the church had kept up involvement in the cultic and immoral life of the city (6:14–7:1; 12:2–13:2).
- Paul was still receiving criticism for his policy of not taking money from them but choosing rather to support himself.
- Worst of all, the church in Corinth had been infiltrated by a group of false apostles who seriously undermined Paul's authenticity as an apostle and thus his authority in the lives of the believers there.

11. In late AD 55 or early AD 56, in view of these developments, Paul sits down to write his fourth letter to the Corinthians. This letter is what we know as 2 Corinthians. We will call it "Corinthian Letter D," a letter Paul hoped would prepare the Corinthian church for his third and final visit (2:2–3; 9:4; 10:2; 11:9; 12:14, 20–21; 13:1–2, 7, 10).

12. In the summer or fall of AD 56, Paul makes his third visit to Corinth, where all is well. It is from Corinth at this time that he writes the epistle to the Romans. "It is probable that this letter [i.e., Romans], his most carefully structured statement, arose out of the issues raised by his most recent problems with the Corinthians, as more hastily expressed in 2 Corinthians. Did Romans have its genesis in lectures given in Corinth in the light of the recent problems there?"[5]

That, in a dozen easy steps, is the sequence of events in the up-and-down relationship between Paul and the church at Corinth. In all, Paul wrote four letters to the church, only two of which God providentially preserved for us in the New Testament:[6]

- Corinthian Letter A: written in AD 54; now lost (1 Cor. 5:9–11).
- Corinthian Letter B: written in late AD 54; our 1 Corinthians.
- Corinthian Letter C: written in the summer of AD 55; commonly called the "severe" or "tearful" letter (2 Cor. 2:4, 9); now lost.
- Corinthian Letter D: written in late AD 55 or early AD 56; our 2 Corinthians.

Thus we see that Paul wrote 2 Corinthians after he received the good news of how the Corinthians had responded to the severe letter (2 Cor. 7:5ff.). Paul is ecstatic that the church had repented and had even taken disciplinary action against the man who had opposed him. He must still on occasion explain his travel plans, the nature of his apostolic authority, and even issue a few warnings and rebukes. But even all this is couched in joy and confidence that the church in Corinth is growing and maturing in Christ.

The Literary Integrity of 2 Corinthians

Even a cursory reading of 2 Corinthians reveals that chapters 1–9 differ markedly in tone and emphasis from chapters 10–13. In 1–9 there is joy, confidence, encouragement, and a generally positive spirit. By contrast, in 10–13 we find harsh rebuke, cutting irony, sarcasm, doubt, and an unmistakable feeling that the situation in Corinth is desperate. How do we account for this radical difference between chapters 1–9 and chapters 10–13? Several theories have been proposed, the more popular of which are as follows.

Some insist that the differences between 1–9 and 10–13 are not radical at all. Although they address different subjects, the disparity between them has been exaggerated. To the degree that proponents of this view acknowledge the emotional differences between 1–9 and 10–13, they attribute it either to a sleepless night before Paul wrote 10–13, or the "mercurial temperament" of the apostle (he wrote 1–9 when he was "up" and 10–13 when he was "down")!

Others argue that chapters 1–9 constitute one letter to the Corinthians and chapters 10–13 yet another. The former were written first in response to the good news brought by Titus, and chapters 10–13 were composed considerably later when Paul received word that the Corinthians had regressed and were again up to their old tricks. On this theory, it is argued that the two different letters were combined as one at some later date to give us what we know as 2 Corinthians.[7]

The most likely explanation is that when Titus arrived with good news from Corinth, Paul immediately sat down and began the letter, writing the first nine chapters. Its completion, however, was perhaps delayed for weeks, or even longer. "Most of us, after all," D. A. Carson explains, "have occasionally put off finishing a letter, doubtless a letter a good deal shorter than 2 Corinthians. In this case, however, Paul may well have received additional news, bad news about the Corinthian church, before he had finished the letter; and if so, this would account for the abrupt change of tone at the beginning of chapter 10. In short, after finishing the first nine chapters, but before actually terminating the letter and sending it off, Paul receives additional bad news, and therefore adds four more chapters of rebuke. Second Corinthians is thus a formally unified letter, but does reflect a substantial change of perspective in the last four chapters."[8]

Conclusion

This collection of meditations on 2 Corinthians was written with the same goal and audience in mind as were the three that preceded it:

The Hope of Glory: 100 Daily Meditations on Colossians; To the One Who Conquers: 50 Daily Meditations on the Seven Letters of Revelation 2–3; and *More Precious than Gold: 50 Daily Meditations on the Psalms.* My intention in each of the books is to provide short but substantive analysis and application of the biblical text, suitable for use as daily devotionals, small group guides for study of God's Word, or even as a commentary in preparation of Sunday school lessons, Bible studies, or sermons. However you may use this volume, I can confidently say that I wrote it "for your joy" (2 Cor. 1:24), that you may find ever-deeper and more long-lasting satisfaction in the glory and sufficiency of Jesus Christ.

Father of Mercies, God of All Comfort

2 Corinthians 1:1–3

Paul, an apostle of Christ Jesus by the will of God, and Timothy our brother,

To the church of God that is at Corinth, with all the saints who are in the whole of Achaia:

Grace to you and peace from God our Father and the Lord Jesus Christ. Blessed be the God and Father of our Lord Jesus Christ, the Father of mercies and God of all comfort.

On August 1, 2007, the I-35W bridge near downtown Minneapolis collapsed. Countless people still suffer both physically and emotionally in the aftermath of this devastating event. Some lost family members in this tragedy. Others' lives were spared, but they were hospitalized with a variety of injuries. Those not directly involved, but perhaps friends with those who were, struggled to make sense of what occurred, asking questions such as, "Where was God? Who *is* God?" What did the church in that city most need to know about God on that tragic day?

There are any number of answers to that question. Some in Minneapolis needed to know that not so much as a sparrow falls to the ground apart from our Father in heaven (Matt. 10:29). They, therefore, being "of more value than many sparrows" (v. 31), may rest assured that this event did not catch God by surprise.

Others needed to be gently and lovingly reminded that none of us knows "what tomorrow will bring" (James 4:14a). Indeed, "What is your life? For you are a mist that appears for a little time and then vanishes" (v. 14b). Instead, they and we "ought to say, 'If the Lord wills, we will live and do this or that'" (v. 15).

And certainly everyone should stand with confidence and unshakable assurance on this glorious truth, that God orchestrates all things, both blessing and blight, both triumph and tragedy, for the ultimate spiritual good of those who love him and "are called according to his purpose" (Rom. 8:28).

But perhaps most important of all, the church in Minneapolis and all the saints throughout Minnesota needed to know what Paul believed the church "at Corinth" together "with all the saints" who were "in the whole of Achaia" needed to know (2 Cor. 1:1), namely, that "the God and Father of our Lord Jesus Christ," who is most worthy of the affirmation and proclamation "blessed," is "the Father of mercies" and the "God of all comfort" (2 Cor. 1:3) "who comforts us in all our affliction" (2 Cor. 1:4).

Paul didn't write this in some isolated ivory tower or from the perspective of a detached and out-of-touch theologian who himself had never encountered pain and suffering and the confusion that tragedy so often elicits. He knew what it was like to endure "affliction" and to be "so utterly burdened" (2 Cor. 1:8) beyond one's strength that the only option left seemed to be death (v. 9). He had tasted the bitter dregs of "deadly peril" (v. 10) and was well acquainted with the darkness of depression (2 Cor. 7:5–6).

This is a man who had suffered the physical horror of being stoned by an angry mob (Acts 14:19) and had felt the relentless emotional pressure of responsibility for the welfare of others (2 Cor. 11:28). This is a man who had endured "far more imprisonments" and "countless beatings" and was "often near death" (2 Cor. 11:23). Five times he had been thrashed with thirty-nine blows and three times beaten with rods, not to mention having endured shipwreck and countless other dangers from both friend and foe (2 Cor. 11:25–26). He knew "toil and hardship" and sleepless nights, even hunger and exposure to the elements (2 Cor. 11:27).

So, when Paul the "apostle of Christ Jesus by the will of God" (2 Cor. 1:1) describes our heavenly Father as one who is the source of mercy and the fount of all comfort, we need to take heed, for he knows of what he speaks.

I suppose some in Minneapolis were inclined to curse God for what transpired in 2007. But as counterintuitive as it seems, Paul declares him "blessed" (2 Cor. 1:3), as one to be thanked and adored and praised! One would almost think Paul had read the book of Job: "Then Job arose and tore his robe and shaved his head and fell on the ground and worshiped. And he said, 'Naked I came from my mother's womb, and naked shall I return. The LORD gave, and the LORD has taken away; *blessed* be the name of the LORD" (Job 1:20–21).

There are two things in particular on which we need to focus in this passage. First, when Paul says that God is the "Father *of* mercies" and "God *of* all comfort," he means more than simply that mercy and comfort come from God. Yes, God most assuredly dispenses these wonderful blessings, but Paul is more concerned to tell us something about God's character, his personality, the disposition and inclination of his heart. In other words, we should read this passage something along the lines of: "the Father *who is characterized by* mercy" and "the God *whose heart delights in* giving comfort."

Yes, of course Paul is describing what God does. But even more foundational is what he says concerning who God is or what he is like. This is his nature, Paul says, his personality, not simply his performance. What God does is a reflection of who he is, and he is above all else characterized by tenderhearted compassion and gentleness and love and a passionate desire to encourage and strengthen those who are suffering hardship and hurt.

The second thing to note is the comprehensive scope of God's merciful and compassionate nature, for he is the "God of *all* comfort, who comforts us in *all* our affliction . . ." (2 Cor. 1:3–4). The former phrase points to the fact that comfort *of every kind* comes from the heart of our Father. Whatever sort of comfort is needed, whatever its nature, you can trust God to be in plentiful supply. Murray Harris suggests that the word "all" may have a "temporal connotation, 'ever ready to console' (TCNT), 'whose consolation never fails us!' (NEB, REB); it may also denote the comprehensiveness of God's compassion, 'who gives every possible encouragement' (NJB). In accordance with his limitless compassion (cf. Ps. 145:9; Mic. 7:19), God provides his people with never-failing comfort of every variety (cf. Isa. 40:1; 51:3, 12; 66:13)."[1]

And just how does God do this? What could he possibly say to us that would have this effect? Perhaps he brings to mind David's declaration: "I say to the LORD, 'You are my Lord; *I have no good apart from you*'" (Ps. 16:2). Or maybe Asaph's affirmation: "Whom have I in heaven but you? And *there is nothing on earth that I desire besides you*" (Ps. 73:25). Or Paul's promise: "*Who shall separate us from the love of Christ?* Shall tribulation, or distress, or persecution, or famine, or nakedness, or danger, or sword, [or collapsing bridges]? No, in all these things we are more than conquerors through him who loved us" (Rom. 8:35, 37).

I can't begin to know what those in Minneapolis were and still are suffering, and I certainly don't intend to pontificate with pious words spoken from the comfort and safety of my own circumstances. But this I do know and can say with all confidence: "The steadfast love of the Lord never ceases; *his mercies never come to an end*; they are new every morning; great is your faithfulness. 'The Lord [not physical life or health or wealth] is my portion,' says my soul, 'therefore I will hope in him'" (Lam. 3:22–24).

Conduits of Divine Comfort

2 Corinthians 1:3–7

Blessed be the God and Father of our Lord Jesus Christ, the Father of mercies and God of all comfort, who comforts us in all our affliction, so that we may be able to comfort those who are in any affliction, with the comfort with which we ourselves are comforted by God. For as we share abundantly in Christ's sufferings, so through Christ we share abundantly in comfort too. If we are afflicted, it is for your comfort and salvation; and if we are comforted, it is for your comfort, which you experience when you patiently endure the same sufferings that we suffer. Our hope for you is unshaken, for we know that as you share in our sufferings, you will also share in our comfort.

One thing that I've never heard said is that people profit the most from those who suffer the least. The most profound and lasting encouragement typically emanates from people who've experienced the deepest trials and greatest loss. When I'm hurting or wallowing in self-pity, I don't instinctively turn to those who've been insulated from pain or who've never tasted the bitter dregs of disappointment and heartache. People who've walked through "the valley of the shadow of death" and bear its scars are a greater inspiration to me than all the collective wisdom of those who remain safely isolated on the mountaintop of spiritual triumph.

However, this isn't something widely embraced in our day. All too often we look on the healthy and wealthy and conclude they must be walking in lockstep with the Lord, while those who struggle and suffer and endure an endless succession of heartaches are deficient in faith and therefore disqualified from any meaningful ministry to others.

Two of my heroes are a standing rebuke to such unbiblical thinking. Few have had a greater impact on my life than the Soviet dissident author Aleksandr Solzhenitsyn and quadriplegic Joni Eareckson Tada. The former endured the injustice of Stalin's gulag and the persecution of an atheist communist regime while the latter has spent the last forty or so years in a wheelchair. Yet their endurance and joy and resolute commitment to Christ have inspired millions, myself included.

There's a sense in which they've been *conduits of divine comfort*, middlemen, so to speak, "between producer and consumers,"[1] much like the apostle Paul described himself in 2 Corinthians 1:3–7. This calls for explanation.

Let's not be naïve. Solzhenitsyn and Tada, again like Paul, have each undoubtedly felt the pressure to yield to self-pity and bitterness. After all, few things have the power to turn us in upon ourselves as do affliction and inexplicable suffering. When we hurt, we rarely think of others. We expect them to think of us.

Both Solzhenitsyn and Tada openly confess to their initial, indeed recurring, struggles with suffering. There have been times when they both prayed for death, wanting only to be delivered from an anguish that at times seemed senseless and unjust. I suppose some today would consider them failures, decidedly lacking in faith. How else, after all, does one explain their pain and constant battles? Surely this couldn't be "God's will," or could it?

Reflect for a moment on your own seasons of suffering, and consider the two most likely questions that came to mind: "Why me?" and "Doesn't anyone care?" The first is directed at God and implicitly accuses him of injustice. The second is aimed at others and explicitly charges them with insensitivity. But as I read this

26

paragraph in 2 Corinthians 1, I hear Paul saying that there are two quite different questions that ought immediately to cross our lips: "Who else?" and "What for?"

I want to highlight two remarkable truths found in 2 Corinthians 1:3–7. There are undoubtedly other things that could be said, but let's focus on these two in particular, in reverse order.

First, Paul clearly affirms that there is what can only be called a qualitative and quantitative *correspondence* between the intensity of human suffering and the availability of divine comfort. If there is an abundance of suffering, so too there is a supply of comfort that is more than adequate to sustain the hurting soul (see esp. v. 5).

No amount of human suffering can outstrip or exceed the resources in God's heart to bring comfort and sustenance and grace to see us through. You need never doubt whether God is up to the task of providing what your soul most needs to survive, even thrive, in the midst of the worst imaginable heartache and hardship. It was only because Paul was confident that God's comfort matched and exceeded his suffering that he was able to mediate that comfort to others when they faced similar, perhaps even more severe, trials.

Second, Paul also discerned a *divine design* in his hardship. What might appear haphazard and serendipitous to the human eye comes wrapped in the package of God's eternal purpose. Look closely at Paul's statement in verse 4 where he asserts that when God comforts us "in all our affliction" it is "*so that* we may be able to comfort those who are in any affliction, with the comfort with which we ourselves are comforted by God." Pain threatens to anesthetize us to any observable "so that." It seems so senseless, so random, so utterly lacking in good and devoid of a goal. But Paul won't hear of it. Whatever degree of suffering I've endured, the apostle says, it was *to equip me to serve you* who likewise endure affliction of body and anguish of soul.

This doesn't immediately resonate with many of us. We are by nature so intractably selfish that we regard our own souls "as the center of all providences" and "naturally seek to explain everything by its bearing on ourselves alone."[2] We struggle to envision how our pain and hardship could possibly have any relevance for or bearing upon anyone else. If nothing else, Paul's confession "calls into

27

question the individualism of modern Christianity and the sense of remoteness within and among many contemporary churches."[3]

But there's a vital lesson for us to learn in this truth. When faced with affliction, whatever its nature or source or perceived cause, stop and do two things: first, avail yourself of the corresponding comforts of Christ and, second, lift up your head, look around, and ask, "Who else, Lord?"

Here's how Paul put it in terms of his relationship to the Corinthians. "If we are afflicted, it is *for your* comfort and salvation; and if we are comforted, it is *for your* comfort, which you experience when you patiently endure the same sufferings that we suffer. Our hope *for you* is unshaken, for we know that as you share in our sufferings, you will also share in our comfort" (2 Cor. 1:6–7). Nothing in Paul's life was interpreted as existing or occurring solely for himself. It was *for them!*

There are two possible ways to interpret Paul's use of the word "salvation" in verse 6. Certainly he is not claiming that his sufferings are redemptive, as if he accomplished in his body and soul what only Christ achieved at the cross. Rather, some believe Paul is afflicted for their "salvation" in the sense that they received the gospel in the context of his suffering. "What they tend to despise in him [his weakness that comes from suffering] is part and parcel of what brought life to them."[4] On the other hand, the word "salvation" may simply refer more to their general well-being—their spiritual safety and health as well as joy and victory over sin (i.e., sanctification) rather than any notion of deliverance from divine wrath.

In any case, as Murray Harris rightly notes, "Paul's suffering of affliction and endurance of trial ultimately benefited the Corinthians in that he was thereby equipped to administer divine encouragement to them when they were afflicted and to ensure their preservation and spiritual well-being when they underwent trial."[5]

I'll be honest: I've never found obedience to this passage an easy thing. To look up and away from my own discomfort to take note of others for whose sake God is equipping me runs counter to my instinctive fixation with self. That's why I must constantly be reminded: God's comfort is more than adequate to meet my needs so that he may meet the needs of others through me.

So, I hope the next time I hurt or am confused or perhaps am put upon unjustly, I'll not ask, "Why me, Lord?" but rather, "Who else?" Then, from the deep reservoir of abundant and wholly adequate strength that God supplies, I'll become a conduit for the life-giving, refreshing waters of divine comfort for which others so desperately thirst.

3

God's Design in Our Distress

2 Corinthians 1:8–11

For we do not want you to be ignorant, brothers, of the affliction we experienced in Asia. For we were so utterly burdened beyond our strength that we despaired of life itself. Indeed, we felt that we had received the sentence of death. But that was to make us rely not on ourselves but on God who raises the dead. He delivered us from such a deadly peril, and he will deliver us. On him we have set our hope that he will deliver us again. You also must help us by prayer, so that many will give thanks on our behalf for the blessing granted us through the prayers of many.

L et me provide a brief sketch of Paul's experience so that we might have a framework for understanding the profound spiritual lessons that follow.

Sometime between the writing of 1 Corinthians and 2 Corinthians, most likely no earlier than the spring of AD 55 and no later than the summer or fall of AD 56, Paul had what he considered a singular and altogether unique brush with death that transformed his perspective on life and ministry and, above all, his relationship with God.

Twice in verse 8 he uses a word, best translated "beyond" (*huper*), that indicates he viewed this experience as unparalleled. When one recalls his statement in Philippians 4:13 ("I can do all things through him who strengthens me"), what he describes in 2 Corinthians must assuredly have been in a category unto itself in terms of its severity and potential for ending Paul's life.

Paul uses vivid, if not shocking, terms to describe the depths of despair to which he was subjected: he was "so utterly burdened," and the affliction was "beyond our strength" to endure. The word translated "despaired" is a compound verb, the components of which "point to the total . . . unavailability . . . of an exit . . . from oppressive circumstances, a situation prompting not so much acute embarrassment as unnerving despair."[1]

Scholars have long speculated on the nature of this affliction. Was it a literal and quite physical confrontation with "beasts" in the arena at Ephesus (1 Cor. 15:32)? Was it the life-threatening circumstances of the riot at Ephesus, instigated by Demetrius the silversmith (Acts 19:23–41)? Was it exposure to extraordinary persecution and peril from his enemies, or perhaps a sentence of death passed against him by a civil court, or possibly some unidentified hardship like extended hunger or a near-death experience during the course of one of his many imprisonments?

I'm convinced that Paul has in view some recurrent illness, a painful and obviously life-threatening affliction, the burden of which was so severe as to expel all hope of survival. Of course, we'll never know for sure. What's most important is how it transformed Paul's perspective on life and the lessons we should learn from it as well.

We should also note that the word translated "sentence" (*apokrima*) of death in verse 9 appears only here in the New Testament and might be rendered "response" or "answer" or something similar. This suggests that while in the throes of this horrific affliction Paul made inquiry, either of himself or of God, to which the reply came: "You will die!" Of course, we don't know any of this for certain, but one thing is clear: Paul didn't die at that time and was convinced that God would deliver him yet again in the future from comparable encounters with death (v. 10). So Murray Harris is probably right in saying that "the divine verdict must have signified something like,

31

'Not death now, but ultimately death from a similar *thlipsis*'" (i.e., "affliction").[2]

Whether we face physical illness or financial stress or relational disappointments, we find it hard to see in it anything remotely approaching a "purpose" or "reason." Such disillusioning experiences strike us as random and senseless and lacking all value. Often the best we can do is write it off as an attack of the enemy, never discerning the divine design in our distress.

But as overwhelming, excessive, and burdensome as this brush with death was for Paul, *he knew that God was in it!* The point of it all, Paul says, "was to make us rely not on ourselves but on God who raises the dead" (v. 9). For those who regard all such anguish and suffering as pointless, this may come as a considerable shock.

One can almost hear Paul saying to himself before he ever said it to the Corinthians: "I've grown too self-reliant. I've become accustomed to trusting in my own charisma, my education, my reputation, my depth of theological insight. I'm dangerously close to taking credit for what only God can do. I'm on the brink of blasphemy! This is no small matter. Trusting in oneself is an affront to God, and he won't have it!"

How far will God go to ensure that Paul doesn't trust in himself and his own skills and spiritual savvy? How seriously does God regard this tendency in the human heart, whether Paul's or yours or mine? To what lengths will he go to guarantee that he alone gets the glory? In Paul's case, God knocked out every man-made prop and reduced him to utter despair. Said God: "Paul, it matters immensely to me that you not look to yourself for strength or rely on your own ingenuity. If there was ever any doubt in your mind concerning this, consider your condition. If I don't intervene and deliver you, you will most assuredly die!"

"Oh, come on, Sam. It can't be that big of a deal, can it?" Well, let's consider what *self-reliance* says: "God, I'm more capable than you are of accomplishing this task. God, I'm wiser than you are in figuring out how this should be done. God, I'm more adept than you are at sorting through options and discerning the proper path to follow. God, I'm more deserving than you are of the credit and praise for fulfilling this ministry from which so many stand to profit."

No one has expressed this more vividly and to the point than James Denney. What he writes is truly profound:

> It is natural . . . for us to trust in ourselves. It is so natural, and so confirmed by the habits of a lifetime, that no ordinary difficulties or perplexities avail to break us of it. It takes all God can do to root up our self-confidence. He must reduce us to despair; He must bring us to such an extremity that the one voice we have in our hearts, the one voice that cries to us wherever we look round for help, is death, death, death. It is out of this despair that the superhuman hope is born. It is out of this abject helplessness that the soul learns to look up with new trust to God. . . . How do most of us attain to any faith in Providence? Is it not by proving, through numberless experiments, that it is not in man that walketh to direct his steps? Is it not by coming, again and again, to the limit of our resources, and being compelled to feel that unless there is a wisdom and a love at work on our behalf, immeasurably wiser and more benign than our own, life is a moral chaos? . . . *[O]nly desperation opens our eyes to God's love.*[3]

The explicit "in order that" of verse 9 (NAS; ESV renders it "but that was to") ought forever to silence those who doubt whether God is sovereign over the troubles and afflictions of life. There is always design in our distress. God so values our trust in him alone that he will graciously dismantle everything else in the world that we might be tempted to rely on: even life itself, if necessary. His desire is that we grow deeper and stronger in our confidence that he himself is all we need.

Some are bothered by this, believing that God's orchestration of Paul's affliction was a high price the apostle was forced to pay by an insensitive and selfish God whose only concern was to glorify himself. May it never be!

God's seeking his glory in Paul's trust was the most loving and tenderhearted thing he could ever have done for the apostle! For in orchestrating these events to undermine Paul's self-reliance, God made it possible for Paul to find satisfaction in the One who will never fail or falter or prove untrustworthy.

There is incomparable joy for our souls in learning to rest in God, not ourselves, in experiencing divine strength, not human weakness. Paul's affliction, as severe and unsettling as it initially may have been (or even continued to be), was the most effective way to lead him to drink from a reservoir of rest and delight and sustaining grace that will never run dry. Whatever was done to wean Paul from himself and cultivate confidence in God alone must be regarded as the highest and most heartfelt expression of love imaginable.

4

Prayer: Dealing with Our Doubts

2 Corinthians 1:11

You also must help us by prayer, so that many will give thanks on our behalf for the blessing granted us through the prayers of many.

If you've ever had doubts about the importance and power of prayer (and all of us have), this passage is for you.

Paul has just confidently declared that the God who already delivered him from a life-threatening affliction would do so yet again (2 Cor. 1:10). God's purpose in Paul's suffering had worked: he no longer looked to himself but now trusted wholly in the "God who raises the dead" (v. 9).

I can just hear some conclude from this: "Well, what then is the point of prayer? If Paul is so confident that God 'will deliver' (v. 10) him, it matters little, if at all, whether the Corinthians pray. God's going to do what God's going to do irrespective of their prayers for Paul or, conversely, their indifference toward him. Whatever will be, will be."

That may well be some people's conclusion, but I assure you it wasn't Paul's! No sooner has he spoken with assurance of God's gracious intentions toward him than he enlists the intercessory prayers of the Corinthians on his behalf. What is it that Paul asks them to ask God? Undoubtedly he encourages them to ask God to do what God has declared is his desire and character to do! Does that sound odd? Perhaps, but there it is in black and white.

God will deliver us, Paul says. We have put our hope in him "that he will deliver us again" (v. 10). Therefore, based on this assurance, flowing out of this confidence, we beseech you Corinthians to "help us" (v. 11) by praying for our welfare.

Some have argued that the opening line of verse 11 should be rendered with a conditional force: "*If* you help us by your prayers" or "provided that you, for your part, help us by interceding on our behalf." If we follow this suggestion, and I think we should, it would serve to reinforce the emphasis Paul consistently places on prayer as a contributing factor to the success of his ministry (see below on Philem. 22, Phil. 1:19, and Rom. 15:30–32).

His desire was that news of his rescue from death be the impetus for the saints in Corinth to join together in prayer on his behalf, in response to which he hoped God would deliver him yet again should similar perilous circumstances arise. If a "blessing" or "favor" (NAS) was to be granted Paul, if his ministry was to continue with success, these believers must intercede on his behalf. And not only would he prosper as a result, God also would be glorified by the many thanksgivings that were uttered for the blessings he bestowed on Paul through prayer.

Do you see how prayer is always a win for all concerned? Look at the dynamics of intercession, how it works for the benefit of everyone involved:

- The ones who pray (in this case, the Corinthians) experience the joy of being an instrument in the fulfillment of God's purposes and delight in beholding how God works in response to their intercessory pleas (cf. Rom. 10:14–15).
- The one who is prayed for (in this case, the apostle Paul) experiences the joy of being delivered from peril or sustained

in trial or being made the recipient of some otherwise unat-
tainable blessing.
- The one to whom prayer is offered (in every case, God) experiences the joy of being thanked, and thus glorified, for having
intervened in a way that only God can in order to bless or
deliver or save his people.

Thus what we read in 2 Corinthians 1:11 is similar to the emphasis found elsewhere in Paul's writings. On two occasions he indicated
that whether or not he would be released from prison may well be
dependent on prayer. Although the power to set him free appeared
to rest with the civil authorities, they were but instruments used
by God to accomplish his purpose in Paul's life (see Prov. 21:1), a
purpose God had determined to fulfill by means of prayer offered
by the saints on Paul's behalf.

In his letter to Philemon, Paul wrote, "At the same time, prepare
a guest room for me, for I am hoping that *through your prayers* I will
be graciously given to you" (v. 22). The word here translated "given"
means "to graciously grant a favor." This, combined with the fact
that he writes in the passive voice, indicates that Paul envisioned
his physical welfare and eventual whereabouts to be ultimately in
God's hands. And God, Paul hoped, had determined to respond to
the petitions of his people, specifically Philemon and his household,
to secure Paul's release.

Paul was uncertain of the outcome. He hoped to be set free, but
knew that the matter rested with God. The civil authorities in this
case were mere intermediaries who could be moved to do God's
bidding in response to the petitions of God's people. Is it too much
to say that without their prayers, Paul had no hope? Is it too much
to say that had Philemon and his family not prayed, Paul may well
have remained in that prison? Perhaps God had purposed to secure
Paul's release through another means should the saints have faltered
in their prayers for him. Perhaps. But not to pray on that assumption
would have been presumptuous and sinful on the part of Philemon
and his household.

We find a similar scenario described in Philippians 1. Paul is again
confident of his impending release from prison and ultimate vindica-
tion. Yet he also says, "for I know that *through your prayers* and the

help of the Spirit of Jesus Christ this will turn out for my deliverance" (Phil. 1:19). Paul evidently believed that God had purposed to effect his deliverance through the prayers of the Christians at Philippi and the gracious provision of the Holy Spirit.

Paul's appeal to the Roman Christians is especially poignant:

> I appeal to you, brothers, by our Lord Jesus Christ and by the love of the Spirit, to strive together with me in your prayers to God on my behalf, that I may be delivered from the unbelievers in Judea, and that my service for Jerusalem may be acceptable to the saints, so that by God's will I may come to you with joy and be refreshed in your company. (Rom. 15:30–32)

The apostle was convinced that God had suspended the success of his journeys and mission on the prayers of his people. Without those prayers, Paul was at a loss. His anxiety about a threat from the unbelieving Jews in Judea was well-founded (see Acts 20–21). Therefore, "his request for continued prayers was not merely a tactical maneuver to engage their sympathy, but a call for help in what he knew to be a matter of life and death."[1]

His plan to come to Rome and enjoy the fellowship of these saints was also dependent on prayer (see 1 Thess. 3:10–13). Important here is Paul's statement in Romans 15:32 where he suspends his impending journey on "God's will." He refused to presume on God's determinate purpose, never suggesting that he will make it to Rome whether or not the saints choose to pray for him. Paul eventually made it to Rome, although his arrival there was not in the manner he expected (see Acts 21:17–28:16). In any case, the important thing to note is that Paul believed in the power and importance of prayer as a means employed by God in the effectual fulfillment of his will.

Simply put, we must never presume that God will grant us apart from prayer what he has ordained to grant us only by means of prayer. We may not have the theological wisdom to fully decipher how prayer functions in relation to God's will, but we must never cast it aside on the arrogant and unbiblical assumption that it is ultimately irrelevant to God's purpose for us and others.

Here's the bottom line: If we don't ask, God doesn't give. If God doesn't give, people don't receive. If people don't receive, God won't be thanked. Think about it. Better still, pray about it.

5

When Christians Misunderstand Christians

2 Corinthians 1:12–2:4

For our boast is this, the testimony of our conscience, that we behaved in the world with simplicity and godly sincerity, not by earthly wisdom but by the grace of God, and supremely so toward you. For we are not writing to you anything other than what you read and acknowledge and I hope you will fully acknowledge—just as you did partially acknowledge us—that on the day of our Lord Jesus you will boast of us as we will boast of you. . . .

And I wrote as I did, so that when I came I might not suffer pain from those who should have made me rejoice, for I felt sure of all of you, that my joy would be the joy of you all. For I wrote to you out of much affliction and anguish of heart and with many tears, not to cause you pain but to let you know the abundant love that I have for you.

No one enjoys being misunderstood or having his motives called into question. We can get fairly feisty when others question our integrity in this way, especially if we know in the depths of our heart that we intended only good.

We are all by nature defensive, but there are different ways of going about vindicating our reputation or explaining our aim. All too often we react, rather than respond, and we do so in anger and bitterness at those who've dared to express doubts about our sincerity. No one modeled godly self-defense more clearly and consistently than the apostle Paul, and nowhere is it seen more explicitly than in this passage that closes the first chapter of 2 Corinthians.

Paul had numerous enemies in Corinth, men who were determined to criticize his every move and undermine the church's confidence in his apostolic credentials. In these verses we detect at least three accusations brought against him: (1) his conduct in verse 12; (2) his correspondence in verses 13–14; and (3) his course of travel in 1:15–2:4.

I want to skip the first two of these and focus on the third. I'll return to this paragraph in subsequent meditations to address other matters Paul raised that are profitable for us today.

It's important to understand the actual sequence of events as a framework for making sense of Paul's response to his critics.

Contrary to the accusations of his opponents, Paul did not change his itinerary because he was fickle or unstable, far less because he cared little for the Corinthians but only for himself; indeed, he changed his plans *for their sake.*

Paul had hoped to visit the Corinthians twice: first, on his way to Macedonia, and second, on his way back from Macedonia (see vv. 15–16). This changed, however, when Timothy arrived in Corinth bearing the letter we know as 1 Corinthians and discovered how bad things were. Upon hearing of this, Paul immediately made an urgent visit to Corinth, a visit that was confrontational as well as humiliating and bitter for him (see 2:1). Paul quickly returned to Ephesus and determined not to make another painful visit to Corinth. Therefore, he called off the double stop he had earlier planned. It was this alteration in his plans that opened him up to the charge of being fickle and unstable.

Paul's seemingly arbitrary change of plans, the Corinthians insisted, was motivated by self-interest and a lack of concern for them. They charge him with making plans like a worldly man, according to the mood of the moment (see vv. 17–18).

James Denney explains what Paul must have been feeling:

Am I . . . in my character and conduct, like a shifty, unprincipled politician—a man who has no convictions, or no conscience about his convictions—a man who is guided, not by any higher spirit dwelling in him, but solely by considerations of selfish interest? Do I say things out of mere compliment, not meaning them? When I make promises, or announce intentions, is it always with the tacit reservation that they may be canceled if they turn out inconvenient? Do you suppose that I *purposely* represent myself . . . as a man who affirms and denies, makes promises and breaks them, has 'Yes, yes, and No, no,' dwelling side by side in his soul? You know me far better than to suppose any such thing. All my communications with you have been inconsistent with such a view of my character. As God is faithful, our word to you is not Yes and No. It is not incoherent, or equivocal, or self-contradictory. It is entirely truthful and self-consistent.[1]

I'll return to verses 19–22 in a later meditation, but here I only take note of Paul's vigorous denial that he is a man given to vacillation and insensitive disregard for the people entrusted to his care. He's not the sort who says "yes" one moment, only to reverse himself on some inexplicable, self-serving whim and then declare "no."

Paul is a man of his word, as is the God whom he loves and serves (v. 18). The Father doesn't assure us of some great blessing, only to withdraw it, without justification, to serve his own interests. When God makes a promise to his people, he fulfills it in Christ. This, Paul says, is the pattern and principle on which he has based his ministry to the Corinthians. One can almost hear him say, no doubt with great energy and passion: "How could I possibly preach to you the good news of a God who always acts with your best interests at heart and never fails to fulfill his promises, and then turn around and treat you with utter disregard by behaving in a double-minded and self-serving way?"

Of course, in the final analysis Paul cares little what they think of him so long as they put their trust wholly in Christ. It may even be that Paul is telling them here, "If you refuse to believe me, at least remember the truth and consistency of my message concerning God's gracious work in you through his Son. You may consider me untrustworthy, but you can hardly question the veracity and fidelity

41

of God as revealed in Jesus. And ultimately it is only with the latter that I'm concerned."

In any case, Paul will again insist in the remainder of this paragraph (1:23–2:4) that he made his decision based on his undying love for the Corinthians, his concern for their spiritual welfare, and, above all, for the sake of their joy in Jesus (see esp. v. 24).

As I said earlier, we'll return to these verses in a subsequent meditation, but here I want to identify several important lessons for us in the way Paul dealt with this church.

First, don't be quick to "read between the lines." Unless past indiscretions or the preponderance of evidence indicate otherwise, trust your Christian friends. Give them the benefit of the doubt when they say they are sincere (vv. 13–14).

Second, don't always look for some ulterior and sinister motive in what others do simply because things did not turn out the way you wanted them to (vv. 15–16).

Third, if someone has proven himself faithful and devoted in the past, don't be quick to believe accusations brought against him by an outsider. Be patient and give him an opportunity to explain himself. In other words, don't jump to conclusions, for it just may be the case that *you* are the one at fault (vv. 17, 23).

Fourth, don't become frustrated or withdraw yourself from other Christians if they should prove fickle or unfaithful. Ultimately, your trust and dependence are not in them anyway, but in Christ who never fails (vv. 19–22).

Fifth, and finally, even if it means suffering unjustly and being slandered, avoid unnecessary confrontations. Don't be too quick to vindicate yourself. Be willing to endure what you don't deserve for the sake of peace in the body of Christ. The opportunity to clear your name will eventually come (v. 23).

6

It Was Grace That Did It

2 Corinthians 1:12

For our boast is this, the testimony of our conscience, that we behaved in the world with simplicity and godly sincerity, not by earthly wisdom but by the grace of God, and supremely so toward you.

This verse is one more example of those many biblical texts that are typically ignored but carry a powerful word of both rebuke and encouragement to the church. I hardly need remind you of the crisis that exists in pastoral ministry today. Rarely a day goes by that I don't hear of another moral failure or theological compromise. Of course, one wouldn't expect to hear much about that faithful servant who toils silently for the sake of God and his people, most often in a church of fewer than two hundred souls. But regardless of the size or seeming insignificance of many churches, Paul's statement needs to be loudly trumpeted for all to hear.

A quick word of reminder is in order concerning the context of Paul's comment. He is dealing with several accusations that his detractors in Corinth had launched at him. We saw in chapter 5 that some had charged him with being self-serving and unreliable for having changed his plans about making a visit to Corinth (see 1:15–2:4).

Paul also responds to rumors that he was duplicitous and evasive in the way he wrote to the Corinthians (1:13). He wants them to understand that there's no need to read between the lines. There are no hidden meanings or secret agendas in his letters. He writes what he means and means what he writes.

The charge that concerns us here is that Paul was either dishonest or insincere or both, perhaps even given to worldly pragmatism in his conduct and the decisions he made in ministry. There's so much to be gleaned from this one verse, but I'll make just seven observations.

First, don't be put off by the fact that Paul "boasts" (v. 12; this and related terms appear throughout 2 Corinthians: see 5:12; 7:4, 14; 8:24; 9:2–3; 10:8, 13, 15–17; 11:10, 12, 16–18, 30; 12:1, 5–6, 9). Some might immediately conclude that this of itself proves that Paul is of dubious character. However, a closer look at these many texts indicates that he is mimicking the bragging of his opponents and that merely using the terminology is something he finds inherently offensive (see esp. 11:10–12:9).

He's also careful to point out that if he does "boast" it is only "in the Lord" (10:17; 11:17). In fact, as we'll note below, he explicitly traces the source of his "simplicity" (or possibly "holiness") and "sincerity," on the basis of which he "boasts," to the grace of God, not his own fleshly efforts. Thus when Paul "boasts" of these virtues, in view of which he has a clean conscience, he is obviously boasting in what God has done by sheer grace alone (see 1 Cor. 1:31; 2 Cor. 10:17).

Second, Paul labored with a clean conscience, both in terms of his relation to the world in general and to the Corinthians in particular. Of course, conscience alone is inadequate. Self-delusion is always a threat. Only the Lord ultimately can judge what's in the heart (see 1 Cor. 4:4–5; 2 Cor. 5:10). This mention of his conscience, therefore, is "a reference to the objective work of God in his life as manifest in his outward behavior."[1] Paul is confident that his conduct is consistent with the intent of his heart.

Third, Paul was quick and clear to the effect that whatever "simplicity" and "sincerity" he displayed came from God. Literally, both of these virtues are "of God" (the ESV renders it "godly sincerity"). Some argue this should be rendered "before God" or "in the sight of God," while others follow the ESV and insist that these qualities are God-like or "godly" in nature. While either is possible, I think Paul is stating starkly that he isn't ultimately or personally responsible for his virtuous conduct: God is. Paul will willingly take credit for his failures, but only God is to be praised for his success. This confirms, as noted above, that whatever "boasting" Paul does is in celebration of what God has accomplished through him.

Fourth, Paul's life and ministry were characterized by "simplicity." Some manuscripts read "holiness" (*hagioteti*), but I believe the more accurate reading is "simplicity" (*haploteti*). Paul is the only New Testament author to use this word, and five of its eight occurrences are here in 2 Corinthians (1:12; 8:2; 9:11, 13; 11:3; also see Rom. 12:8; Eph. 6:5; Col. 3:22).

Would that pastors and leaders everywhere might heed this example! Paul knew that few things were more destructive to Christ-exalting ministry than duplicity and deviousness. With Paul there was a singularity of purpose, a single-minded commitment, a simplicity of devotion that he refused to compromise. Isn't it amazing what simple honesty can do to adorn the gospel, and how one deceitful deed can undermine it!

Fifth, Paul conducted all of his dealings with absolute transparency, or what the ESV calls "sincerity." Murray Harris has pointed out that this word (*heilikrineia*) is derived from "*heile*" (the sun's heat) and "*krino*" (I judge), "denoting the state of something which has survived the searching and searing light of the sun, 'judged by the sun's splendor/heat'; thus 'sincerity,' 'ingenuousness.'"[2]

Perhaps we all need to pause, put life on hold for a moment, and subject our souls to the searing, searching light of God's analysis. If we were to do so, what would be revealed? Pride? Fear? Secret agendas? Self-promotion? Greed? Or perhaps (again, only "by the grace of God") a life and approach to ministry that is wholly above-board, self-effacing, Christ-exalting, and as devoid as can be this side of heaven of hypocrisy and superficiality.

Sixth, much of the church today is infected with "earthly wisdom": be it pragmatism ("if it works, do it—regardless of whether it is biblical"), compromise ("cutting corners doesn't matter, so long as giving increases and our building program succeeds"), or elevating cultural trends and preferences above the truths of God's Word ("after all, we don't want to offend anyone; they might not come back next week").

Seventh, and finally, Paul draws a stark and vivid contrast between "earthly wisdom" or human cleverness on the one hand, and "divine grace" on the other. Either you live by man's wisdom, according to the dictates and desires of human nature, or you are energized by God's gracious power.

It's important to note that Paul envisioned his entire existence, both in public and private, whether in the mundane affairs of life or in the ministry he discharged at Corinth and elsewhere, as being energized and sustained and guided by "the grace of God." His conduct or behavior was governed by the power of God's gracious presence.

The word "grace" in this verse is not a reference merely to a principle by which God operates among us or even the truth that he saves us according to his kind intentions in Christ rather than on the basis of alleged good works. Grace is God's sustaining, empowering energy through the Holy Spirit that enabled Paul to resist the temptation to boast of his own accomplishments or trust in his own insights or yield to the pressure to conform to the world's expectations.

If Paul was single-minded, it was grace that did it! If Paul was sincere, it was grace that did it! If Paul was governed by God's will and not the ways of the world, it was grace that did it!

Some find it easier and more appealing to capitulate to the pressure and fashion their ministries according to the latest Gallup poll. Standing resolute and firm against the fashionable trends of religious life in America is hard. Setting Scripture to the side and tickling the ears of one's audience requires less effort and often reaps greater rewards. But Paul will have nothing of it, and neither should we.

7

Yes!

2 Corinthians 1:18–20

As surely as God is faithful, our word to you has not been Yes
and No. For the Son of God, Jesus Christ, whom we proclaimed
among you, Silvanus and Timothy and I, was not Yes and No, but
in him it is always Yes. For all the promises of God find their Yes
in him. That is why it is through him that we utter our Amen to
God for his glory.

There are times when I think people have given the citizens
of Corinth a bad rap. I know I've been guilty of it. When in
need of an example of sin run amok, or immaturity, or theological ignorance, I've often pointed at Corinth. Poor chaps. Yet the
more I think about it, the more convinced I am that they probably
weren't much different from the rest of us. Yes, I know, there was
division in the church there, not to mention immorality, ambition,
and spiritual pride. Like I said, they weren't much different from
the rest of us.

One of their biggest problems was lack of trust, in both God
and their leaders. We've already noted their suspicions about Paul.
"*Apostle* Paul? Well, we're not too sure about that," they might have
been overheard saying. "If he were truly *apostolic* and really cared

about us, why did he change his travel plans and leave us in a lurch?" Paul answers that question, and puts their fears to rest here in 2 Corinthians 1:12–2:4.

He does his best to assure them that he is not the sort who says "yes" when he really means "no," the sort who is casual about his promises and thinks only of himself. "We strive to be consistent," Paul says, "because God is. We prize faithfulness and integrity in our relationship with you because that's how God treats all of us."

In the final analysis, if the Corinthians can't bring themselves to trust Paul, he wants to make sure that they trust Christ. "I'm not perfect," says the apostle. "But he is. His word to you is marked by integrity and sincerity, and his promises will never be withdrawn or fall short of fulfillment. When it comes to who he is and what he's said, he's an unequivocal yes!"

What a powerful reminder to forgetful folk. What a marvelous affirmation to suspicious souls. What a rock-solid reassurance concerning God's intentions toward us. When we doubt his word or let anxiety supplant faith, we are called to look at Christ Jesus and behold God's indelible "Yes!"

Because of Jesus Christ—the perfection of his life, the sufficiency of his death, the power of his resurrection, the certainty of his return—God's answer to your questions is always and ever, "Yes!"

"God, will you answer me when I call (Ps. 4:1)?" Yes!

"God, will you be my refuge in the face of my enemies (Ps. 7:1)?" Yes!

"God, can you actually make known to me the pathway of life (Ps. 16:11)?" Yes!

"God, will you be for me fullness of joy and pleasures evermore (Ps. 16:11)?" Yes!

"God, can I count on you to be my rock and my fortress and my deliverer, my shield and my stronghold (Ps. 18:2)?" Yes!

"God, will you be there with me and for me and beside me, as I walk through the valley of the shadow of death (Ps. 23:4)?" Yes!

"God, will you satisfy my heart with ravishing revelations of your beauty (Ps. 27:4)?" Yes!

"God, if I delight myself in you alone, will you truly grant me the desires of my heart (Ps. 37:4)?" Yes!

"God, does your steadfast love endure all day long (Ps. 52:1)?" Yes!

"God, will you be the strength of my heart and my portion forever (Ps. 73:26)?" Yes!

"God, what of your promise not to deal with me according to my sins or repay me according to my iniquities (Ps. 103:10)? Is that really true?" Yes!

"God, is it true that your mercies never come to an end? Are they literally new every morning (Lam. 3:22)?" Yes!

"God, will you continue to sing over me with joy and delight, in spite of my brokenness and weakness and immaturity (Zeph. 3:17)?" Yes!

"God, are you really committed to orchestrating all things in my life for my ultimate spiritual good (Rom. 8:28)?" Yes!

"God, will you always comfort me in my affliction so that I may be equipped and qualified to comfort others in theirs (2 Cor. 1:4)?" Yes!

"God, are all the spiritual blessings in heavenly places already and absolutely mine (Eph. 1:3)?" Yes!

"God, will you always be present to do for me far more abundantly than all I can ask or think (Eph. 3:20)?" Yes!

"God, if I work out my salvation with fear and trembling, can I know with unassailable confidence that it is you who is already at work in me to will and to do for your good pleasure (Phil. 2:12–13)?" Yes!

"God, if I pour out my heart to you with thanksgiving, will your peace guard my heart now and forever (Phil. 4:6–7)?" Yes!

"God, is it still the case that you plan on sanctifying me wholly, in spirit and soul and body (1 Thess. 5:23)?" Yes!

"God, are you actually committed to never leaving me or forsaking me (Heb. 13:5)?" Yes!

"God, if I draw near to you, will you really draw near to me (James 4:8)?" Yes!

"God, if I confess my sins, will you forever be faithful and just and forgive me of them (1 John 1:9)?" Yes!

Yes!

"God, is it still your intent to wipe away every tear from my eyes and to banish pain and sorrow and death (Rev. 21:4)?" Yes!

"God, are you coming soon (Rev. 22:20)?" Yes!

I want to believe you, God. I long to trust your promises. How can I know for sure? To whom can I look for assurance? What guarantee will you provide?

Jesus! For all God's promises find their Yes in Christ!

8

Cinderella No More

2 Corinthians 1:21–22

And it is God who establishes us with you in Christ, and has anointed us, and who has also put his seal on us and given us his Spirit in our hearts as a guarantee.

Theologian Alister McGrath once identified the Holy Spirit as "the Cinderella of the Trinity. The other two sisters," he said, "may have gone to the theological ball; the Holy Spirit got left behind every time."[1] My, my, how times have changed! Contemporary interest in the person and ministry of the Spirit is unparalleled in the history of the church. As a result, passages such as 2 Corinthians 1:21–22 are being given renewed attention. It's hard to imagine two verses anywhere in Scripture that speak more directly and powerfully of the work of the Spirit than these.

I want to draw our attention in this passage to three glorious truths concerning the Spirit, the third of which is the primary focus of this meditation.

First, God the Father has "anointed" us with the Spirit, even as he anointed Jesus. Paul deliberately juxtaposes two words to highlight this remarkable truth. Here is a translation that makes the point unmistakably:

It is God who establishes us with you in Christ (*christon*) and "christed" (*chrisas*) us.

Or again:

It is God who establishes us with you in *the anointed one* and *anointed* us.

Thus, just as Jesus said of himself, "the Spirit of the Lord is upon me, because he has anointed me" (Luke 4:18), likewise Christians are spoken of as anointed ones because we too have received the same Holy Spirit and are thus set apart and empowered to serve God and authorized to act on his behalf. The Spirit who indwelt and energized the ministry of Jesus indwells and energizes us! All Christians, therefore, are *anointed* (as confirmed also in 1 John 2:20–21, 27).

Second, God has "sealed" us with his Spirit. As Paul said in Ephesians 1:13, "In him you also, when you heard the word of truth, the gospel of your salvation, and believed in him, were sealed with the promised Holy Spirit" (see also Eph. 4:30).

The term "seal," when used literally, referred to a stamped impression in wax pointing to ownership and protection. When used metaphorically, it meant (1) to authenticate (see John 3:33; 6:27; 1 Cor. 9:2) or confirm as genuine and true, including the idea that what is sealed is stamped with the character of its owner; (2) to designate or mark out as one's property; to declare and signify ownership (see Rev. 7:3–8; 9:4); or (3) to render secure or to establish (i.e., protect; see Eph. 4:30; Matt. 27:66; Rev. 20:3).

With what, precisely, are we sealed? Both Ephesians 1:13 and 4:30 would appear to suggest that the seal is the Spirit himself, "by whom God has marked believers and claimed them for his own."[2] In other words, it isn't so much that the Spirit *does* the sealing as the Spirit *is* the seal (although it certainly could be both). Hence, sealing is nothing less than the reception and consequent indwelling of the Holy Spirit.

Third, God the Father has "given us his Spirit in our hearts as a guarantee." Before we explore this word translated "guarantee" (or "pledge"), I want to draw attention to something all Christians experience.

I have in mind that ill-defined but inescapable ache in your heart for something better, that instinctive sense that all is not as it should be, that there is a world yet to come where justice will prevail, and truth will be known, and peace will reign, and all will love righteousness, and beauty will radiate and permeate everything. You know what I'm talking about. One struggles to put it in words. It's as if you've been allowed to smell the flower but not see it, taste the feast but not consume it.

I suppose there are even times when we'd just as soon not at all be aware, even in the slightest degree, of the "not yet" in God's redemptive purposes. The frustration in knowing it is coming but not seeing it is often more than one can endure. It would almost be better never to have caught a glimpse of the glory to come than to have seen it but be compelled to continue life in its absence. But then we come to our senses. "Of course I'm glad to have touched the reality of future glory, if only in part, if only in a passing glance, if only in a gentle twinge in my spirit that says, 'Wait, be patient, it will be worth it all.'"

Where does it come from, this unfulfilled confidence in what is not yet, this unconsummated longing for what we can't see? It's as if we are given just enough water to sustain us in the desert, with the ever echoing reassurance that an oasis of unimaginable and transcendent refreshment is just beyond our grasp.

It comes from the deposit of the Holy Spirit in our hearts! On three occasions Paul describes the Spirit as the *down payment*, the *pledge*, or as the ESV renders it here in 2 Corinthians 1:22, the *guarantee*. The term (*arrabon*) itself was used in commercial transactions to refer to the first installment of the total amount due. The down payment effectively guaranteed the fulfillment of whatever contractual obligations were assumed. "The Spirit, therefore," says Gordon Fee, "serves as God's down payment in our present lives, the certain evidence that the future has come into the present, the sure guarantee that the future will be realized in full measure."[3] John Eadie's explanation beautifully sums up Paul's point:

> It is the token that the whole sum stipulated for will be given when the term of service expires. The earnest is not withdrawn, but is supplemented at the appointed period. . . . But the earnest, though it

differ in degree, is the same in kind with the prospective inheritance. The earnest is not withdrawn, nor a totally new circle of possessions substituted. Heaven is but an addition to present enjoyments. Knowledge in heaven is but a development of what is enjoyed on earth; its holiness is but the purity of time elevated and perfected; and its happiness is no new fountain opened in the sanctified bosom, but only the expansion and refinement of those susceptibilities which were first awakened on earth by confidence in the Divine redeemer. The earnest, in short, is the "inheritance" in miniature, and it is also a pledge that the inheritance shall be ultimately and fully enjoyed.[4]

In giving the Holy Spirit to us, writes Peter O'Brien, "God is not simply promising us our final inheritance but actually providing us with a foretaste of it, even if it 'is only a *small fraction* of the future endowment.'"[5]

In other words, when you become consciously and experientially aware of the presence within of transcendent deity, of a joy that is inexpressible and full of glory, of a power that triumphs over the allure of fleshly lusts, of a delight that is sweeter than the passing pleasures of sin, of a satisfaction that puts earthly success to shame, you are sensing, if only in small measure, what will be yours in infinite and unending degree in the age to come!

It is nothing less than the precious Spirit of God quickening your soul to the reality of what awaits us on the other side, assuring you that he is here, "in our hearts" (2 Cor. 1:22), to *guarantee* that all God has promised will come to pass. We have it on no less authority than the Holy Spirit himself that what we sense in our spirit now is a foretaste of what we will see and hear and feel and taste and enjoy throughout the ages to come in all the fullness of God himself.

Even so, come Lord Jesus!

9

For Joy

2 Corinthians 1:23–2:4

But I call God to witness against me—it was to spare you that I refrained from coming again to Corinth. Not that we lord it over your faith, but we work with you for your joy, for you stand firm in your faith. For I made up my mind not to make another painful visit to you. For if I cause you pain, who is there to make me glad but the one whom I have pained? And I wrote as I did, so that when I came I might not suffer pain from those who should have made me rejoice, for I felt sure of all of you, that my joy would be the joy of you all. For I wrote to you out of much affliction and anguish of heart and with many tears, not to cause you pain but to let you know the abundant love that I have for you.

Do you fight for joy? Do you think of joy as something to be sought as the object of diligent striving and focused labor? Or do you think of it more as an aftereffect, a by-product of other and more important pursuits? Or am I splitting hairs, leaving you to wonder, *Sam, what difference does it make?* I think we should let Paul answer that question.

As we've already noted on several occasions, Paul goes to extraordinary lengths to explain why he changed his plans about visiting

Corinth. Here at the close of chapter 1 and the start of chapter 2, he again accounts for his behavior and in doing so pulls back the curtain, so to speak, on his own heart and exposes the driving force in his life and ministry.

Some in Corinth felt that Paul's behavior and change of travel plans was indicative of an arrogant and authoritative style of leadership. But the apostle is quick to remind them that it was neither indifference to their needs nor pompous posturing that governed his actions. Rather, he made his decisions based on what he believed would best serve their *joy*! Look again closely at verse 24—"we work with you *for your joy*."

The two verses at the close of chapter 1 deserve close attention. Obviously, Paul is concerned that his comments in verse 23 might lead to a false conclusion. His words, "not that" or "this is not to say" is his way of introducing a clarification of what has preceded, lest they draw an unwarranted inference from what he had said. Paul apparently fears that his statement about wanting to "spare" them (v. 23) could be misunderstood, as if he were presuming to have such authority over their lives that their every move was subject to his control or that his every move impacted their lives. "No," Paul says. "I have no intention of trying to tyrannize your faith, nor could I even if I wanted to, for your faith rests in the power of God, not in me or the wisdom of any human being" (see 1 Cor. 2:5).

Ultimately, the Corinthians, as is true of all believers (including you), are accountable to God alone. Although they may have come to faith *through* Paul's ministry, their faith is *in God*, not in an apostle or a pastor or an elder or a teacher or a theologian. "You have only one Lord," Paul says, "and it ain't me" (or something similar; see Rom. 14:4).

Both 1 and 2 Corinthians must have been difficult for the church to swallow. Paul had some harsh things to say to the church in Corinth (deservedly so, I might add). His rebukes often stung. He pulled no punches and cut no corners. As far as Paul was concerned, compromise was the language of contempt. If you love someone, you speak the truth, no matter how painful or discomfiting it may be. But in every case, beneath and behind every word in every verse in every chapter, Paul's aim was the same: joy!

Unlike so many in his own day and even more in ours, Paul didn't discharge his apostolic calling to expand his personal power or to broaden his influence or to bolster his reputation or to increase his control, far less to pad his bank account, but to intensify their joy in Jesus.

Paul can almost be heard to say, "Whether I'm rebuking you for sectarianism in the church (1 Corinthians 3) or laxity in moral conduct (1 Corinthians 5–6) or abuse of spiritual power (1 Corinthians 12–14), my aim is your joy in Jesus. Whether I appeal to you to be financially generous (2 Corinthians 8–9) or warn you of false apostles (2 Corinthians 11), my aim is your joy in Jesus."

Should Paul have been pressed for an explanation, he would have said: "I aim to intensify their joy because apart from their souls relishing and resting in the all-sufficiency of Jesus Christ, they don't stand a chance against Satan." I believe he would have answered like the good Christian Hedonist that he was: "I work for your joy because God is most glorified in you Corinthians (and all believers) when you are most pleased and satisfied and enthralled with the plenitude of divine beauty seen only in the face of Jesus Christ."

Let's be clear about one thing: the joy for which Paul labored and prayed and preached should never be thought of in terms of "feeling good about yourself" or living in the lap of luxury. This joy is far and away removed from any form of self-indulgent smugness or that superficial psychological giddiness that comes from reaping the material comforts of western society.

The joy that Paul has in mind is a deep, durable delight in the splendor of God that utterly ruins you for anything else. It is a whole-souled savoring of the spiritual sweetness of Jesus that drives out all competing pleasures and leads the soul to rest content with the knowledge of God and the blessings of intimacy with him. This is the kind of joy that, rather than being dependent on material and physical comfort, actually frees you from bondage to it and liberates you from sinful reliance on worldly conveniences and gadgets and gold.

Paul's commitment to their joy in Jesus was motivated, at least in part, by his belief that Satan was no less committed to their joy in the passing pleasures of sin (see Heb. 11:25). He knew all too well that the diabolical strategy of the enemy is to seduce us into believing that the world and the flesh and sinful self-indulgence can do for our weary and broken hearts what God can't (or won't).

This is the battle that we face each day. We awaken to a world at war for the allegiance of our minds and the affections of our souls. The winner will be whoever can persuade us that he will bring the greatest and most soul-satisfying joy. That is why Paul labored and prayed so passionately and sacrificially for joy in Jesus in the hearts of that first-century church.

To reinforce his point, he tells them in the opening verses of chapter 2 that if he had visited them when he had first planned to do so it would only have led to the diminishing of their joy and thus the deprivation of his own. "If I had come at that time," Paul says, "I would have been compelled to deal with your unrepentant sin. It would have been unprofitably painful for you. And if you are in anguish, your joy is lessened. And if your joy is lessened, so too is mine in you." This is why Paul delayed his trip, namely, to give them opportunity to put their house in order so that upon his arrival their joy in Jesus might enrich his, and his joy in Jesus might in turn enrich theirs.

As you consider your involvement in the lives of others or your ministry to the broader body of Christ, do you consciously think in advance, What can I do to help them set aside obstacles to full and lasting satisfaction in Jesus? What can I do to portray the glory and beauty of Christ so that the allure of the world, the flesh, and the devil loses its luster? How can I live that others might see in me the superior pleasures that are found in Christ alone?

I awakened this morning, as did you, and as the Corinthians did each day of their lives, with an unshakable, inescapable, relentless longing for joy. I can't wash it from my skin in the shower or hold my breath in hopes that it will disappear. Psychological catharsis will not drive it from me. Willpower will not suppress its influence. And contrary to much so-called "Christian" counsel, I should not exorcise its presence or pray for its defeat.

Paul's counsel to them and to us, I believe, is to pursue God's presence where "fullness of joy" may be found (Ps. 16:11), to "taste and see that the LORD is good" (Ps. 34:8), to drink from the river of his delights (Ps. 36:8), and to avail ourselves of every means possible to increase and intensify our delight and satisfaction in him who is joy incarnate.

10

Reflections on Church Discipline

2 Corinthians 2:5–11

Now if anyone has caused pain, he has caused it not to me, but in some measure—not to put it too severely—to all of you. For such a one, this punishment by the majority is enough, so you should rather turn to forgive and comfort him, or he may be overwhelmed by excessive sorrow. So I beg you to reaffirm your love for him. For this is why I wrote, that I might test you and know whether you are obedient in everything. Anyone whom you forgive, I also forgive. Indeed, what I have forgiven, if I have forgiven anything, has been for your sake in the presence of Christ, so that we would not be outwitted by Satan; for we are not ignorant of his designs.

I know this may be a stretch for many of you, but I'd like to ask that you meditate with me on the subject of church discipline. That's right, church discipline. The fact that your immediate and instinctive response is probably somewhat (or considerably) negative reflects how far removed we are today from the spirit of the New Testament. As we'll see, a commitment to discipline in the local church is indicative not only of one's love for holiness, as well as those lingering in sin, but most of all for the Lord Jesus who "gave himself up for her [i.e., the church], that he might sanctify her, having cleansed her by the washing of water with the word, so that he might present the church to himself in splendor, without spot or wrinkle or any such thing, that she might be holy and without blemish" (Eph. 5:25–27).

There is considerable debate among commentators as to the identity of the individual in 2 Corinthians 2:5–11. Some older commentaries insist that this is the incestuous man of 1 Corinthians 5. More recent commentators argue that this is the person who opposed Paul and worked to undermine his apostolic authority. This man "may have been connected with the sexual aberrations in Corinth that involved a number of people and that appear to have necessitated Paul's recent unscheduled visit (12:21–13:2). It is quite possible that the man also supported the practice of ongoing attendance at temples in the city (6:14–7:1), despite Paul's warnings in the First Letter (1 Cor. 10:14–22). . . . Perhaps this man resisted Paul's admonitions to the Corinthians during his second visit and was himself the major reason that visit was so painful for Paul."[1]

In any case, the church had imposed discipline upon him, most likely by prohibiting his presence at the Lord's Table and withdrawing routine fellowship. The good news is that it worked! "For such a one," Paul says, "this punishment by the majority is *enough*." He had evidently repented, and Paul now calls for a reaffirmation of love for him and his restoration into the life of the church.

Paul is concerned lest immoderate severity destroy this man. Thus he encourages the Corinthians "to forgive and comfort him, or he may be overwhelmed by excessive sorrow." The tendency of human nature is to hold the offender at arm's length, to forgive but not forget, to say "I receive you back," but to treat the person like a leper. Philip Hughes reminds us that "discipline which is so inflexible as to leave no place for repentance and reconciliation has ceased to be truly Christian; for it is no less a scandal to cut off the penitent sinner from all hope of re-entry into the comfort and security of the fellowship of the redeemed community than it is to permit flagrant wickedness to continue unpunished in the Body of Christ."[2]

Let's approach this topic by asking and answering a series of five questions.

First, why is church discipline so neglected, if not ignored altogether, in our day? Perhaps the principal cause is a pervasive ignorance of biblical teaching on the subject. Many believe that church discipline is infrequently mentioned in Scripture and therefore unimportant; others are ignorant of the purpose of discipline and see it only as destructive to people.

Another factor is calloused insensitivity toward sin, a failure to take seriously the offense of sin, or a tendency toward unsanctified mercy in our treatment of the unrepentant. Undoubtedly the spirit of individualism also plays a role. We have lost the sense of community and mutual responsibility one for another. How often has it been said, as a way of justifying our passivity toward sin, "Well, it's not really any of my business, is it?" Discipline is costly because my brother's/sister's business now becomes mine.

A misapplication of our Lord's words in Matthew 7:1 ("Judge not, that you be not judged") has certainly put hesitancy in the hearts of many in regard to dealing with sin in the local church. The fear of rejection also comes into play; many fear that the offending party will say, "Mind your own business. You have no authority to tell me what I can and can't do."

I strongly suspect that fear of legal reprisal in the form of lawsuits has paralyzed many. Many people (even church leaders) simply dislike confrontation. Talking directly about personal sin with an offender is difficult; it makes us feel uneasy and uncomfortable, so why rock the boat? Many think that if we simply ignore the problem, in time it will go away. "Time heals all," or so they contend.

I've known instances where discipline stalled from fear of driving the person away, especially if the offender is a major financial contributor to the church! Related to this is the fear of dividing and ultimately even splitting the church over whether and how and to what extent discipline should be applied (invariably many think the discipline was too severe, while others are convinced it was too lenient).

Many struggle with a false concept of discipline because of observed abuses. They associate discipline with heresy hunts, intolerance, oppression, harshness, mean-spiritedness, self-righteousness, legalism, and so forth. Related to this is the fear of being labeled a cult if we insist on too strict a code of conduct for our members.

Others resist taking disciplinary steps because it entails change. In other words, the power of tradition is hard to overcome: "We've never done it before, and we've done OK. Why risk messing things up now?"

Second, why is discipline necessary? There are several reasons: (1) to maintain (as far as possible) the purity of the church (1 Cor. 3:17; Eph. 5:25–27); (2) because Scripture requires it (Matt. 18:15–20; 1 Corinthians 5); (3) in order to maintain a proper witness to the world; the church corporately, as with an elder individually, is to have a good reputation with "outsiders" (1 Tim. 3:7); (4) to facilitate growth and to preserve unity in the body (Eph. 4:1–16); (5) to expose unbelievers (1 John 2:19); (6) to restore the erring brother or sister to obedience and fellowship (1 Cor. 5:5; 2 Cor. 2:6–7, 10; Gal. 6:1; 2 Thess. 3:14–15); (7) to deter others (1 Tim. 5:20); (8) to avert corporate discipline (Rev. 2:14–25); (9) because sin is rarely if ever an individual issue; it almost always has corporate ramifications (2 Cor. 2:5). The whole of the body (or at least a large segment of it) is adversely affected by the misdeeds of one member; and (10) evidently Paul believed that the willingness to embrace the task of discipline was a mark of maturity in a church's corporate life (2 Cor. 2:9).

Third, in what instances or for what sins should we exercise church discipline? Unrepentant moral evil, as in the case of the incestuous man of 1 Corinthians 5, would certainly qualify. Divisiveness and serious doctrinal error are also mentioned in the New Testament (Rom. 16:17–18; Titus 3:9–10). Paul also speaks of more general, unspecified transgressions in Galatians 6:1 as calling for disciplinary intervention (see also 2 Thess. 3:6–15).

Fourth, how are we to do discipline? Matthew 18:15–17 recommends the following steps:

- First, private rebuke (Matt. 18:15). Do it gently, in love, out of compassion, seeking to encourage. The purpose for private rebuke is to resolve the problem without fueling unnecessary gossip.

- Second, if private rebuke is unsuccessful, plural rebuke (Matt. 18:16; see also Deut. 17:6; 19:15; Num. 35:30). The "others" in Matthew 18:16 might perhaps be church leaders, people who know the offender, or people who know of the sin.
- Third, if plural rebuke is unsuccessful, public rebuke (Matt. 18:17).
- Fourth, if public rebuke is unsuccessful, "excommunication" (Matt. 18:17; 1 Cor. 5:11; Titus 3:10; possibly 2 Thess. 3:14).
- Fifth, if repentance occurs, restoration to fellowship and reaffirmation of love (2 Cor. 2:6–8; Gal. 6:1).
- Sixth, Matthew 18:18–20 affirms that whatever decision is made in the matter, whether the offending person is "bound" or "loosed," it reflects the will of God in heaven. When a church is united in its application of discipline, it can rest confidently in God's promise that he will provide wisdom and guidance for making the correct decision. Thus, the verdict of heaven, so to speak, is consonant with that of the church, before which the matter was adjudicated.

Fifth, who should administer discipline? Certainly the elders of the church are to take the initiative and provide general oversight for the process (see Acts 20:28–32; 1 Thess. 5:14; Heb. 13:17). But the congregation as a whole must also be involved (2 Cor. 2:6). This latter text raises the question of whether there may have been a minority in Corinth who dissented from the action taken.

In sum, the motivation for discipline is *love* (for the errant believer) and the goal of discipline is *restoration*. If Christ himself is so passionately committed to the purity of the church that he would sacrifice his life on her behalf in order to present her "to himself in splendor, without spot or wrinkle or any such thing . . ." (Eph. 5:27), we can hardly afford to turn a blind eye to repeated and unrepentant sin in our midst. May God grant us the grace and wisdom so essential for this delicate and crucial task.

11

Satanic Stratagems

2 Corinthians 2:11

So that we would not be outwitted by Satan; for we are not ignorant of his designs.

W hen it comes to the life and unity of the body of Christ, Satan is anything but a passive, innocent bystander. Although he may be invisible to the eye and undetected by physical means, you may rest assured that he is present, employing every imaginable device (and some unimaginable) to undermine the integrity of God's people and to sow seeds of discord and confusion. Paul himself was extremely careful and deliberate in how he sought to resolve the problems in Corinth, lest they all "be outwitted by Satan; for we are not ignorant of his designs" (2 Cor. 2:11).

Make no mistake: Satan has a plan. Although sinful, he is not stupid. He does not act haphazardly or without a goal in view. He had "designs" for the church at Corinth, and he most surely does for your congregation today as well. In Ephesians 6:11 Paul referred to the "schemes" (lit., *methodia*, from which we derive our word "method") of the Devil. He has cunning and wily stratagems not only for the individual believer but also for the corporate body of

Christ. It is essential, therefore, that we be aware of them and fully prepared to respond.

Second Corinthians 2:5–11 reveals Satan's determination to incite disunity and division. This appears to be an instance in which Satan seeks to exploit the otherwise good intentions of the church. Certain people in Corinth, ostensibly to maintain the purity of the church, were reluctant to forgive and restore the wayward, but now repentant, brother. This harshness would give Satan an opportunity to crush the spirit of the repentant sinner and drive him to despair, most likely resulting in his being forever cut off from the church.

What are some of Satan's other designs and schemes in both the church and the world?

1. He works in active opposition to the gospel, blinding the minds of unbelievers to keep them from seeing the truth about Christ (2 Cor. 4:4). There are at least two factors in spiritual blindness: fleshly, sinful, self-resistance to the truth on the one hand, and satanic/demonic hardening or blinding on the other. Before we ever arrive on the scene with the gospel, Satan is exerting a stupefying influence on the mind of the unbeliever. In other words, we face more than mere intellectual obstacles. We face supernatural opposition. How does Satan do it? There is any number of possibilities. For example:

- He distracts unbelievers when an opportunity to hear the gospel is at hand: interruptions, day-dreaming, the phone ringing, an emergency of some sort, the sudden remembrance of a job or other responsibility that needs immediate attention, or the intrusion of a friend (see Acts 13:7b–8). Before serious consideration is given, Satan snatches the seed of the gospel (Matt. 13:4, 18–19) from their minds: on the way home from church the car breaks down, or the conversation turns to politics or sports, or a sexy billboard diverts attention, or something on the radio captivates their minds.
- He stirs up hostility and suspicion in the unbeliever's mind concerning the competency and integrity of the person presenting the gospel. The unbeliever suddenly imputes sinister motives to the Christian: "He's in it for the money," or "She only wants to gain control over me," or "He's just looking for

another notch on his Bible so he can boast to others of one more convert." Sometimes the unbeliever will excuse his or her unbelief by questioning the intellectual and academic credentials of the believer: "He or she is so uneducated. What does he or she know anyway?"

- Satan also stirs up non-Christians to distort what is being said into something the speaker never intended (see John 2:19–21; 6:48–52; 7:33–36; 8:51–53). Satan prompts them to draw false conclusions or implications from the gospel that make it seem absurd. He inclines unbelievers' minds to link the believer with people who've disgraced Christianity in the past, giving them an excuse to reject what is being said (i.e., guilt by association): "All you Christians are just like those hucksters on TV! You're in it for the gold and the glory!"

- Satan puts in their minds all sorts of questions and convinces unbelievers that if they can't get completely satisfying answers, Christianity can't be true. Right in the middle of witnessing to someone, he/she suddenly blurts out questions like, "What about evil?" "What about all the hypocrites in the church?" "What about the heathen in Africa?" "Why is there only one way? It seems egotistical." "Why are there so many denominations?"

- Just as the gospel is beginning to make sense, Satan stirs up pride or produces feelings of independence and self-sufficiency: "I don't need a religious crutch. I'm my own man!"

- Satan might suddenly prompt unbelievers to place a higher value on things they might lose if they were to become a Christian: friends, fame, money, fleshly pleasures, approval of others.

- Satan stirs up feelings of hopelessness: "Not even this will work. There's no hope. My life is a lost cause. Not even Jesus can help."

- Satan will do all he can to oppose and disrupt missionary endeavors (1 Thess. 2:18) by disrupting travel plans, influencing the minds of state officials to delay or deny the issuing of visas, inflicting illness, provoking military conflict, and so forth.

2. Satan is often (but not always) the source of sickness (Acts 10:38; Matt. 8:16; Mark 9:17–18; Luke 13:10–17).

3. He can inflict death as well as provoke the paralyzing fear of it (Heb. 2:14; see Job 1:13–19; John 10:10).

4. He plants sinful plans and purposes in the minds of men (Acts 5:3; John 13:2; Matt. 16:21–23). It is instructive to observe that in the case of Acts 5, "it is not through some act of terrible depravity, but through an act of religious devotion, that Satan brings about the downfall of Ananias and Sapphira. . . . It is sobering to think that the very good that God's people attempt to do can be their undoing."[1]

5. On occasion, Satan will himself indwell a person (John 13:27). By speaking of Satan as "entering" Judas, John uses language reminiscent of demonization (see Luke 8:30–33). It is important to note, however, that Judas's motive was also greed, and nowhere is he exonerated from his action simply because he was indwelt by the Devil.

6. He sets a snare or trap for people, perhaps with a view to exploiting and intensifying their sinful inclinations. According to 1 Timothy 3:6–7, Satan is able to exploit any blemish on the reputation of a Christian leader. In 2 Timothy 2:25–26, Paul appears to speak of believers who have been led astray through false teaching. Satan thus strives to hold people captive to do his will by deceiving them to believe what is false and misleading. If nothing else, this text emphasizes how crucial sound doctrine is.

7. He infiltrates the church and plants within it his own people (Matt. 13:37–39).

8. He tests or tries Christians, the malicious "sifting like wheat" of Peter's faith being an excellent example (Luke 22:31). Clearly, Satan is unable to act outside the parameters that God establishes but must first ask permission. He wanted to destroy Peter by inciting him to deny Jesus. But God's intent in permitting Satan to do so was altogether different. God's purposes with Peter were to instruct him, humble him, perhaps discipline him, and certainly to use him as an example to others of both human arrogance and the possibility of forgiveness and restoration. This points to the fact that often we cannot easily say "Satan did it" or "God did it." In cases such as this, both are true (with the understanding that God's will is

67

sovereign, supreme, and overriding), but their respective goals are clearly opposite. Sydney Page's comments concerning this incident are important:

> Luke 22:31–32 reveals that Satan can subject the loyalty of the followers of Jesus to severe tests that are designed to produce failure. So intense are the pressures to which Satan is able to subject believers that the faith of even the most courageous may be found wanting. Satan is, however, limited in what he can do by what God permits and by the intercession of Jesus on behalf of his own [cf. Rom. 8:34; Heb. 7:25; 1 John 2:1]. Furthermore, those who temporarily falter can be restored and, like Peter, can even resume positions of leadership. It is implied that Satan cannot gain ultimate victory over those for whom Jesus intercedes.[2]

9. He incites persecution, imprisonment, and the political oppression of believers (1 Pet. 5:8–9; Rev. 2:10).

10. He is the accuser of the Christian (Rev. 12:10).

11. He performs signs and wonders to deceive the nations (2 Thess. 2:9–11).

12. He seeks to silence the witness of the church (Rev. 12:10–12).

13. He promotes false doctrine (1 Tim. 4:1–3; Rev. 2:24; 2 Cor. 11:1–15).

14. He can manipulate the weather (but not by virtue of his own inherent power; it is only to the degree that God permits, as is clear from Job 1:18–19; see also Mark 4:37–39).

15. He influences the thoughts and actions of unbelievers (Eph. 2:1–2). It is a stunning thought, similar to that in 1 John 5:18, that Satan is at work in and energizes the disobedience of all unbelievers. This does not mean that all non-Christians are demonized, but it does imply that their unbelief and unrighteous behavior are stimulated and sustained by the enemy. Yet they remain morally culpable for their actions.

16. He attacks married believers in regard to their sexual relationship (1 Cor. 7:5). Paul approves of the decision by married couples to refrain from sexual relations to devote themselves to prayer, but only for a season. To abstain entirely for a prolonged period of time

exposes oneself to unnecessary temptation (i.e., lust and the satisfaction of one's sexual desires outside the bonds of marriage). Again, we see here an example of how the enemy takes an otherwise godly intention and exploits it for his own nefarious purposes.

17. He exploits our sinful decisions, most likely by intensifying the course of action we have already chosen (Eph. 4:26–27). Note that Satan is not credited with or blamed for creating anger in the first place. We are responsible for it. Satan's response is to use this and other such sins to gain access to our lives and to expand and intensify our chosen course of behavior.

18. He confronts us with various temptations (1 Chron. 21:1; Matt. 6:13; 1 Thess. 3:5).

Yes, Satan has "designs" and "schemes," which he intends to undermine our enjoyment of all that God is for us in Jesus. May God grant us both the wisdom to discern his stratagems and the strength and resolve to resist him at all times.

12

The Dangers of Triumphalism

2 Corinthians 2:14

But thanks be to God, who in Christ always leads us in triumphal procession, and through us spreads the fragrance of the knowledge of him everywhere.

One of the more not-so-subtle delusions that exists in many corners of the professing Christian church is what I refer to as *triumphalism*. The more technical theological phrase is *over-realized eschatology*.

The bottom line in triumphalism is the belief that the overt and consummate victories that we will experience only in the age to come are available to us now. I'm not saying that we as Christians shouldn't rejoice in the daily victories we experience by virtue of the enthronement of Christ Jesus and the indwelling power of the Holy Spirit. Yes, we have authority over demonic spirits (see Luke 10:17–20). Yes, we have been blessed "with every spiritual blessing in the heavenly places" (Eph. 1:3) and have been "raised" up with Christ and are "seated" together "with him" (Eph. 2:6). We who believe "that Jesus is the Son of God" have overcome the world (1 John 5:5). And Jesus himself promises great and glorious rewards "to the one who conquers" now (Rev. 2:7, 11).

So the last thing I want to endorse or encourage is a defeatism that fails to embrace and act upon every good and glorious blessing secured for us by the Lord Jesus Christ. But where many often go astray is in their claim that such truths necessarily entail visible and irreversible victories in the present that result in a life free from persecution, suffering, or demonic assault. It's the notion that since I'm a "child of the King" I have a right to live in financial prosperity and complete physical health, free from that "groaning" under the lingering curse of the fall that Paul indicates will continue until Christ's return (see Rom. 8:18–25). I'm talking about that often arrogant and presumptuous triumphalism that belittles those whose "lack of faith" has resulted in a lingering, daily struggle from which Jesus came to deliver them.

What I want to articulate is a perspective on the Christian life that celebrates both our legitimate spiritual triumphs and our ongoing daily trials. Nowhere in Scripture is this dynamic tension more evident than in 2 Corinthians, where Paul speaks of being "afflicted in every way, but not crushed" and of being "perplexed, but not driven to despair" and of being "persecuted, but not forsaken" (2 Cor. 4:8–9). The life he envisions is one in which we "always" carry about in ourselves "the death of Jesus, so that the life of Jesus may also be manifested in our bodies" (2 Cor. 4:10).

Perhaps the best way to explain what I have in mind is found in Paul's description of his own ministry in 2 Corinthians 2:14–17. In verse 14 Paul writes: "But thanks be to God, who in Christ always leads us in triumphal procession, and through us spreads the fragrance of the knowledge of him everywhere." Many will undoubtedly say: "But Sam, there it is! God always leads us in triumph! So why are you so down on triumphalism?" A closer look at what Paul means will help answer that question.

The Greek word translated "triumph" or "triumphal procession" (*thriambeuo*) is used in the New Testament only here and in Colossians 2:15. Most agree that the term refers to the Roman custom in which a victorious general would lead his conquered captives in triumphal procession, often to their execution. However, a number of other interpretive suggestions have also been made.

The King James version of the Bible translates this word as "causeth us to triumph" (a view John Calvin embraced: "Paul means that he had a share in the triumph that God was celebrating"[1]). However, as several others have noted, the accusative following the verb is never the triumphing subject but *always the object of the triumph.*

C. K. Barrett popularized the view that the image is of a victorious general leading his *troops*, not his conquered enemies, through the city streets in a triumphal celebration.[2] According to this view, Paul is one among many soldiers, all of whom are triumphant conquerors.

Some have rendered this, "God triumphs *over us,*" in the sense that all Christian converts are "conquered" by God at conversion. Paul, then, would be alluding to his encounter with God on the Damascus Road. Others acknowledge the imagery of the Roman triumphal procession but limit its application to the shame endured by those who were captured. Thus, Paul is simply identifying himself with the humiliation of those prisoners who were put on parade.

The most probable interpretation is the one that recognizes an obvious paradox in Paul's use of this metaphor. On the one hand, it is God who leads Paul (and by extension, others who likewise preach the gospel as he does) in *triumph*. Yet, on the other hand, to be led in triumph by someone else implies captivity and suffering. Paul Barnett provides this helpful explanation:

> There is paradox here, as implied by the metaphor "lead [captive] in triumph," which points at the same moment to the victory of a conquering general *and* the humiliation of his captives marching to execution. The metaphor is at the same time triumphal and anti-triumphal. It is as God leads his servants as *prisoners of war* in a victory parade that God spreads the knowledge of Christ everywhere through them. Whereas in such victory processions the prisoners would be dejected and embittered, from this captive's lips comes only thanksgiving to God [v. 14], his captor. Here is restated the power-in-weakness theme (cf. 1:3–11) that pervades the letter. . . . [Thus], to be sure, his ministry is marked by suffering, but so far from that disqualifying him as a minister, God's leading him *in Christ* as a suffering servant thereby legitimates his ministry. Christ's humiliation in crucifixion is reproduced in the life of his servant.[3]

72

Thus Paul is not boasting of his victories but compares himself to conquered captives who are being treated rudely and subjected to humiliation while yet in the glorious service of God. Paul asserts that it is precisely in his weakness and suffering as a captive slave of Christ that God receives all the glory as the One who is triumphantly victorious. Compare this passage with how Paul described his apostolic calling in 1 Corinthians 4:9: "For I think that God has exhibited us apostles as last of all, like men sentenced to death, because we have become a spectacle to the world, to angels, and to men."

It was also customary for those being led in this procession to disperse incense along the way. However, the reference to "aroma" (2 Cor. 2:15) and "fragrance" (v. 14, 16) probably also points to the Old Testament sacrifice and the odor of the smoke that ascended to heaven, in which God took unique pleasure. Thus Paul portrays his proclamation of the gospel of Christ as a strong fragrance, "unseen but yet powerful, impinging on all who encounter Paul in his sufferings as he preaches Christ wherever he goes. In the victory parade metaphor of this verse, the apostle is God's captive, whom God leads about spreading the knowledge of Christ—incense-like—by means of the proclamation of Christ."[4] Or again, "as God drags Paul around as his slave, the knowledge of Christ emanates from Paul wherever he goes."[5]

I love Paul's imagery: knowing Jesus is like a sweet aroma! There is a spiritual and emotional pleasure in knowing Jesus that can best be compared to the physical delight we experience when our nostrils are filled with the fragrance of the choicest of perfumes or the soothing aroma of our favorite food. Simply put, *knowing Jesus smells good*, a glorious reality that God makes known through the suffering and struggles of his children.

There is much that is *already* ours, spiritual triumphs to enjoy for which we give unending thanks. But there is also much that we do *not yet* possess, blessings that are reserved for the age to come. It's not always easy to discern when we should, by faith, confidently claim our inheritance, and when we should, in humility, embrace the weakness of living in a fallen world. May God grant us the wisdom to know the difference.

73

13

Smelling Good to God

2 Corinthians 2:15–16

For we are the aroma of Christ to God among those who are being saved and among those who are perishing, to one a fragrance from death to death, to the other a fragrance from life to life. . . .

How do you measure success? By what standard do you assess how well you've done? When you take stock of your life or evaluate the effectiveness of whatever ministry God has given you, how do you determine the outcome? Do you count heads? Or money? Do you apply the criteria typically used in a Gallup poll or Barna survey? Do you size up your efforts as over against those of high-achieving folk in the marketplace or perhaps line up your congregation, side by side, with the megachurch down the road?

All of us are tempted to measure ourselves by comparing what we've produced with that of others, especially those whom we admire or whose names are cited often in the newspaper or on blogs. Let's admit it. We invest far too much in the opinion of the power brokers in our society, whether spiritual or secular. What they think and how well they've done, as well as the size of their facilities and the impact of their ministries weighs heavily on our minds and typically leads to feelings of inferiority and failure.

I can't overemphasize the devastating effects embracing this perspective can bring to the life of the church. It saddens me to see how many have compromised on truth, cutting corners on the gospel or softening the sharp edge of biblical morality in order to enhance one's status or increase attendance or retain the support of some significant donor.

Equally as devastating are those who've abandoned church and ministry altogether, whether from burnout or the unbearable frustration of thinking they've failed God or shown themselves incapable of fulfilling their calling.

If that even remotely resonates in your heart, or if you struggle with feelings of spiritual inferiority, ministerial incompetence, or simple inadequacy as a Christian, heed well the words of the apostle Paul in 2 Corinthians 2:15–16. The biblical standard for "success" articulated in this text is a much-needed remedy for what ails so many in the church today.

Do you want to smell good to God? Then *be true to the gospel!* Be faithful to its terms, articulate its promises, and don't back down from declaring the eternal consequences that come with its denial.

There are two, and *only* two, possible responses to the gospel of Christ. When the message is made known, everyone responds. There is no such thing as neutrality. Indifference or apathy is a myth. Not to believe the good news in Christ Jesus is to reject it. Pretending to ignore it is to deny it.

Either you are among "those who are being saved" or you are among "those who are perishing." The word of the cross is either "folly," utter and absolute foolishness, or it is "the power of God" unto salvation (see 1 Cor. 1:18). The message of Christ that Paul proclaims (and not the messenger) is itself responsible for dividing the hearers in this way.

Wherever, whenever, and to whomever the Christian proclaims the name of Jesus, a fragrance is released. To some it is an aroma of life and hope and renewal and forgiveness. Nothing can compare with the sweet smell of the Son of God. The gospel of his dying and rising for sinners awakens life and leads to life. To others it is a suf-focating, poisonous stench. Charles Spurgeon reminds us:

> The gospel is preached in the ears of all; it only comes with power to some. The power that is in the gospel does not lie in the eloquence of the preacher; otherwise men would be converters of souls. Nor does it lie in the preacher's learning; otherwise it would consist in the wisdom of men. We might preach till our tongues rotted, till we should exhaust our lungs and die, but never a soul would be con-verted unless there were mysterious power going with it—the Holy Ghost changing the will of man. O Sirs! We might as well preach to stone walls as to preach to humanity unless the Holy Ghost be with the Word, to give it power to convert the soul.

But what I want you to see is that Paul is a fragrance to God *regardless* of the response to his message! When, in the midst of suffering, he faithfully proclaims the gospel and is mocked and slan-dered, and the name of Jesus is blasphemed, Paul smells good to God. When, in the midst of suffering, Paul faithfully proclaims the same gospel and is embraced and loved and people bow the knee in love and loyalty to Jesus, Paul smells good to God.

We are a fragrance to God even when our message is rejected. So long as we remain faithful to our commission, we smell good to God. Though our crowds be small and the offering paltry, success is measured by fidelity, not fruit. Whether our efforts lead to "life" or "death," we remain "the aroma of Christ to God" (2 Cor. 2:15). We have succeeded when we preach Jesus truly and biblically.

This will be a difficult pill to swallow only if our fear of man is greater than our fear of God, only if our preference is for man's praise rather than God's. Some of the worst failures in ministry are found in megachurches, where pragmatism often (though not always) trumps principle. Many who appear small in the eyes of man are giants in the kingdom of God. Both success and failure can be found in churches of every size, whether mega or mini.

There's no escaping the fact that you smell, and so do I. May we strive in the power of God's grace to be a fragrant aroma pleasing to him, even if putrid to the world.

14

Is Anyone Sufficient
for These Things? Yes!

2 Corinthians 2:16–17

Who is sufficient for these things? For we are not, like so many, peddlers of God's word, but as men of sincerity, as commissioned by God, in the sight of God we speak in Christ.

A s noted in an earlier meditation, the dangers of triumphalism are very real and imposing. We must resist the temptation to think that faith either insulates us from the trials and struggles and groans of life or elevates us above them altogether. Our "triumph" is precisely in our grace-empowered endurance in the midst of suffering as we faithfully proclaim the gospel, regardless of whether or how many either believe or repudiate the message.

But we must also be extremely careful that we do not draw the wrong conclusions from this, especially in light of Paul's question at the close of verse 16. Following the remarkable description of what constitutes true success in Christian life and ministry, Paul asks the pointed question: "Who is sufficient for these things?" (2 Cor. 2:16). Virtually everyone immediately responds, as they assume humility would require, "No one, certainly not I!"

The reason most think that Paul's question calls for a negative answer is their belief that he has in mind *self*-sufficiency, as if the resources and qualifications for such a ministry are the fruit of one's own wisdom and works. But the word translated "sufficient" carries no such connotations. Paul is, in fact, looking for a *positive* response to his question. "Who is sufficient for these things?" "I am," Paul says, "because I don't peddle the gospel like so many do but rather speak sincerely as commissioned by God and as one who will be judged by God."

There are a couple of reasons for understanding Paul in this way. First, as Scott Hafemann has pointed out, "The language of 'sufficiency' used here alludes to the call of Moses in Exodus 4:10, where in the LXX [Septuagint] Moses responds to God's call by declaring that he is not 'sufficient' (*hikanos* [the same word used here in 2 Cor. 2:16]) for the task. In the context of Exodus 4, Moses is then *made sufficient* by God himself. Paul too sees his sufficiency as coming from God (cf. 2 Cor. 3:4–6)."[1]

Second, observe closely the logical relation between verse 16b and verse 17 as indicated by the word "for" (or "because," sadly omitted in some English translations). Paul is clearly contrasting himself with his opponents who took pride in their personal power and triumphant style of ministry. Unlike them, Paul will say, my ministry originates with God (2 Cor. 2:17), and God has made me adequate for it (2 Cor. 3:6). If Paul were denying his sufficiency for ministry in verse 16, the comparison between himself and the "hucksters" or "peddlers" in verse 17 would make no sense.

How can Paul imply here and assert later (3:6) that he is adequate or sufficient to carry out this ministry and his opponents are not? His answer is direct and to the point: "They peddle the gospel, I don't."

The word translated "peddlers" (*kapeleuo*) is found only here in the New Testament and nowhere in the Septuagint (the Greek translation of the Old Testament). The related noun form (*kapelos*) was virtually synonymous with the idea of a merchant who regularly cheated his customers by misrepresenting his product. According to Murray Harris, this kind of merchant functioned as something of a middle man "between the wholesaler . . . and the general public" who "gained a reputation for manipulating prices or tampering with goods for the sake of profit."[2] Thus the idea is of people who dilute the full strength of the gospel, perhaps eliminating (or at least minimizing) its offensive elements or altering certain theological points, so that the finished "product" will be more appealing to the audience. Their aim was obviously to gain as large a following as possible (not to mention the money that would come with it!).

So, on the one hand, we must resist all expressions of triumphalism while, on the other hand, we must humbly acknowledge and give thanks that God has graciously equipped us as sufficient to disperse the sweet aroma of the knowledge of Christ to a lost and dying world. Therefore, the antidote to arrogant triumphalism isn't defeatism or false humility but the God-given, Christ-centered confidence that is inspired and sustained by him who has qualified us as stewards of the gospel.

Needless to say, Paul's approach to ministry was of a decidedly different origin and character than that of the false teachers and religious hucksters who had infiltrated the congregation at Corinth. He specifically mentions four distinct features of his (and all legitimate) ministry:

> For we are not, like so many, peddlers of God's word, but as men *of sincerity, as commissioned by God, in the sight of God we speak in Christ.* (2 Cor. 2:17)

First, Paul doesn't disguise his true motives in ministry: he speaks with "sincerity," wanting only that people would understand the truth. Whether or not they choose to believe the gospel and live or reject the truth and die is beyond his control. Simply put, he refused to exploit his preaching as a means for personal gain.

Second, he speaks "as commissioned by God" (literally, "as of God"). In other words, what he says originates with God, not himself. He didn't create the gospel. It isn't the product of his imagination nor was it fashioned so as to ensure the greatest possible number of respondents. He speaks only what has been revealed. He is a steward of the truth, not a manufacturer of it (see Gal. 1:11–17).

Third, he speaks "in Christ," from within the spiritual orbit, as it were, and out of the strength and confidence that flows from a vital, living union with Christ.

Fourth, Paul lives and ministers "in the sight of God," by which he means in God's presence, under his omniscient and ever-watchful eye, mindful that God knows every syllable he utters and that he will give a full account to God for what he speaks in God's name. What a remarkably powerful incentive to keep his motives pure and his message orthodox! God was not only the source of Paul's commission, he was also the witness, assessor, and ultimate judge of his work. Paul was not accountable to any human court, least of all the Corinthians, but ultimately to God alone.

It's quite stunning to think, as Hafemann rightly reminds us, that "Paul's entire life as an apostle is contained in these prepositional phrases."[3] So too is yours (and mine). It matters little whether we are students, school teachers, housewives, politicians, or pastors. Our sufficiency is in Christ. Our adequacy comes from him. And thus we can, by the grace of God, and so long as we remain faithful to the terms of the gospel, successfully discharge this stewardship entrusted to us.

Epistles of Christ

2 Corinthians 3:1–3

Are we beginning to commend ourselves again? Or do we need, as some do, letters of recommendation to you, or from you? You yourselves are our letter of recommendation, written on our hearts, to be known and read by all. And you show that you are a letter from Christ delivered by us, written not with ink but with the Spirit of the living God, not on tablets of stone but on tablets of human hearts.

The New Testament describes salvation and our relationship to the Lord in any number of ways, using a variety of images, metaphors, and analogies. Jesus is the Good Shepherd and we are the sheep. God is the giver of life and we are born again. He is the compassionate Father and we are adopted. God is the righteous judge and we are justified. The Spirit is an indwelling presence and we are his temple, and the list could go on.

But one of the more intriguing and instructive images is that of Christians as a *letter* or *epistle* that Jesus himself has written, the Holy Spirit being, as it were, the pen or instrument by which he has authored us. Before we explore this rich metaphor, let me set the context in which it is found.

You will recall that Paul has just defended the integrity of his ministry at the close of 2 Corinthians 2. Unlike those who peddle the Word of God, no doubt for financial gain, he speaks sincerely as one "commissioned by God." He ministers "in Christ" as one who is ever under the scrutiny of God himself (v. 17).

Paul may well have feared that when his enemies heard those words, they would once more accuse him of boasting and self-promotion. Perhaps they would say, "Well, there he goes again, commending himself to you, just like we warned."

The "many" (2:17) who peddled the Word of God are probably the "some" (3:1) who promoted themselves and gained a foothold in Corinth on the strength of letters of commendation. Paul does not altogether deny the validity of using such letters in certain circumstances, but insists that he does not need them when it comes to his relationship with the Corinthians. After all, he had devoted eighteen months to living in Corinth, ministering daily to their needs (see Acts 18:1–11). How could they possibly now require such letters from him before they acknowledged his apostolic office?

Paul's use of the word "again" in verse 1 does not mean he was actually guilty of self-advertisement on some earlier occasion, but simply that his opponents had accused him of it, possibly because of his exhortation in 1 Corinthians 4:16 and 11:1 that they "be imitators of me." But let's take note of Paul's reference to "letters of recommendation."

In my capacity as a pastor and professor these many years of Christian ministry, I have been asked to write dozens of letters of recommendation. Most were on behalf of prospective students seeking admission to a college or university or to a graduate program of study. A few were written as part of their application for employment.

There's nothing wrong with this practice today. The nature of our society and the world of business and education often require it. But in Paul's world the need for letters of recommendation could easily indicate that someone lacked sufficient evidence on his own to back up whatever claims he was making for himself. They were viewed by many, therefore, as "a substitute source of credibility."[1]

Paul's point is that the Corinthians themselves, their very existence as believers and the transformation in their lives, was sufficient recommendation. He didn't need additional proof of the authenticity of his calling. How could the Corinthians yield to the pressure of the false teachers and demand from Paul that he bring with him letters that testified to his apostolic authority? The Corinthians needed only to look at their own experience of Christ to realize that Paul was precisely who he claimed to be and ministered in the power and authority of Jesus himself.

"If it is a letter of recommendation you desire," Paul says, "*you* are it!" In other words, the best evidence of Paul's apostolic credentials is the Corinthian church. As Paul Barnett has said, "The 'letter' written not on paper but in people—the Corinthian messianic assembly—is Christ's visible commendation of Paul, the church's founder. The church is the Lord's commendation of him."[2]

This, then, is the context for the remarkable statement that we find in verse 3. Taking advantage of his earlier reference to "letters" or "epistles" of recommendation, he describes the Corinthians themselves as a "letter" written by Christ! Their conversion is likened to the Lord, through the person and ministry of the Holy Spirit, writing a document that testifies to his glory and beauty and life-changing power!

The implications of this are stunning. Consider, for example, the contemporary discipline known as graphology, perhaps better known simply as handwriting analysis. Although some have questioned its scientific credibility, others contend that the shape, size, and other distinctive features of one's personal script reveal much about an individual's personality and psychological tendencies.

I have no way of knowing if this is true, but it provides a helpful illustration of what happens when a person is born again and begins to grow in conformity to the image of Jesus Christ. My point is that the personality of Christ can be seen in the "letters" that he has graciously written—and we are those letters! Just as the physical dimensions of a person's handwriting may well reveal their character and emotional state of mind, so too the spiritual contours of a Christian ought to manifest the moral beauty of Jesus who has, in a sense, "penned" us.

If we, like the Corinthians, are truly "epistles" written by the gracious hand of Christ himself, we will progressively display his glory and the shape of his personality. If the "epistle" that goes by the name "Christian" is illegible or looks nothing like the person who "penned" them, there is reason to doubt if Christ is truly the saving author of his life. Scott Hafemann is certainly correct when he writes the following:

> In view of Paul's teaching, we simply must not continue to deceive ourselves into thinking that lifestyles of self-serving greed, sexual impurity, self-preserving dishonesty, and prestige-seeking careerism are merely the result of "not yet becoming who we are in Christ." Nothing less than the integrity of our message is at stake in the manner of our lives. Our actions are a manifestation of our moral condition.[3]

The life of faith, Hafemann says, is the work of the Spirit. "But the Spirit does not invade our lives in order to go on vacation! For those in whom the Spirit dwells, we must be able to taste the 'fruit of the Spirit' (Gal. 5:22) or 'the fruit of righteousness' (Phil. 1:11) in our attitudes and actions."[4]

So, what do people discover when they "read" your life? If asked to describe what they learned from the "script of your soul," would they compare it to the *National Enquirer* or some other cheap tabloid? Or would they point to evidence in you of a transcendent scribe, an author whose merciful and gracious penmanship has made himself known in how you speak and live and minister among others?

16

The Surpassing Glory
of the New Covenant

2 Corinthians 3:4–11

Such is the confidence that we have through Christ toward God. Not that we are sufficient in ourselves to claim anything as coming from us, but our sufficiency is from God, who has made us competent to be ministers of a new covenant, not of the letter but of the Spirit. For the letter kills, but the Spirit gives life.

Now if the ministry of death, carved in letters on stone, came with such glory that the Israelites could not gaze at Moses' face because of its glory, which was being brought to an end, will not the ministry of the Spirit have even more glory? For if there was glory in the ministry of condemnation, the ministry of righteousness must far exceed it in glory. Indeed, in this case, what once had glory has come to have no glory at all, because of the glory that surpasses it. For if what was being brought to an end came with glory, much more will what is permanent have glory.

Nothing is more frustrating than knowing what one ought to do and lacking the power to perform it. To see and read and be confronted with the will of God while one is bereft

85

of the resolve and spiritual energy to respond in a positive fashion is my definition of despair!

That is why I thank God daily that I do not live in an age when the law of God was merely written on stone and called for my obedience without the promise of the provision of power. That is why I thank God daily that I have by grace been made a member of the new covenant in Christ Jesus, the distinguishing feature of which is that for every precept there is power and for every statute there is strength and for the otherwise impossible task of saying "yes" to God's commands there is the indwelling presence of the Holy Spirit.

In describing this new covenant of which we've been made members, Paul contrasts it with the Mosaic or old covenant. He associates the new with the Spirit and says that it "gives life," whereas the old he describes as "the letter [which] kills" (2 Cor. 3:6).

This contrast has been misunderstood. It does not mean that the Law of Moses is sinful (see Rom. 7:12–14), nor does it allude to two ways of interpreting Scripture: literal versus spiritual (or allegorical). Far less does it refer to the distinction many make between doctrine and spirit or between mind and heart.

The contrast in view becomes evident when one examines the nature of the new covenant as over against the old. In sum, the Law of Moses was imposed from without on a rebellious people, the result of which was death. The new covenant, on the other hand, is inscribed on the very hearts of its recipients, all of whom, from least to the greatest, will "know the LORD" (Jer. 31:33–34). All participants in the new covenant are provided with the inner power, that is, the Holy Spirit, to fulfill its dictates. The old covenant made no such provision. Its dictates confronted a people whose hearts were stone. The effect of God's commandments on unchanged (stony) hearts is condemnation and death. Thus, spiritually speaking, the old covenant "killed" and made it, therefore, "a ministry of death" (v. 7).

Scott Hafemann provides this excellent summation of Paul's point:

> The problem with the Sinai covenant was not with the law itself, but, as Ezekiel and Jeremiah testify, with the people whose hearts remained hardened under it. The law remains for Paul, as it did for the Jewish traditions of his day, the holy, just, and good expression of

God's covenantal will (Rom. 7:12). Indeed, Paul characterizes the law itself as "spiritual" (7:14). As the expression of God's abiding will, it is not the law per se that kills, or any aspect or perversion of it, but the law *without the Spirit*, that is, the law as "letter." Devoid of God's Spirit, the law remains to those who encounter it merely a rejected declaration of God's saving purposes and promises, including its corresponding calls for repentance and the obedience of faith. Although the law declares God's will, it is powerless to enable people to keep it.[1]

Thus the inadequacy of the Mosaic Law was not due to any inherent sinfulness or failure on its part. Its inadequacy, rather, was that it could only prescribe what people ought to do but could not make provision that would sufficiently enable them to fulfill its commands. The Law of Moses was quite effective in explaining one's moral obligation and exposing one's sin, but it was not endowed with the power to ensure that those who stood under its covenant would fulfill its terms.

So that there should be no doubt concerning the inherent goodness of the old covenant established through Moses, Paul himself speaks of its "glory" no fewer than six times in 2 Corinthians 3:7–11, and no fewer than four times does he refer to the superior "glory" of the new covenant established through Christ!

Before I go any further, let me say a few words about the new covenant. By the way, this is no theological diversion or meaningless bunny trail. This is the foundation for your relationship with God! Nothing could be more personal or important than understanding the terms on which we relate to God as our Lord and Savior and experience the blessings he has provided.

First of all, what is provided for us in the new covenant? According to what we read in Jeremiah 31:31–34 (cf. Ezek. 36:25–28), it provides several glorious blessings, such as the internalization of God's law ("I will put my law within them, and I will write it on their hearts . . ." Jer. 31:33; cf. 2 Cor. 3:3), unbroken fellowship with God ("I will be their God, and they shall be my people," Jer. 31:33), unmediated knowledge of God ("And no longer shall each one teach his neighbor and each his brother, saying, 'Know the LORD,' for they shall all know me, from the least of them to the greatest, declares the LORD . . ." Jer. 33:34), and the unconditional forgiveness of sins ("for I will forgive their iniquity, and I will remember their sin no more," Jer. 31:34).

Second, in whom is the new covenant fulfilled? I'm always a bit stunned that anyone could have any doubts about this, but let me mention five answers that have been given.

Some so-called "classical dispensationalists" argue that the new covenant was given exclusively for ethnic Israel and will therefore be fulfilled only in her at the end of the age when Israel as a nation is saved. The church, according to this view, has no part in the blessings of this covenant.

There have been other dispensationalists who argued that there are two new covenants, one for ethnic Israel and one for the church. Happily, this view has been largely if not altogether abandoned by those who first proposed it.

Still others within the dispensational camp have suggested that there is only one new covenant, for Israel, in which the church shares *spiritually*. In other words, those blessings in the covenant which pertain to salvation are equally enjoyed by the church, but those that pertain to earthly prominence in the land belong solely to Israel.

A fourth view, not very popular but extremely unbiblical and dangerous, is that there are two covenants, one for the Jewish people and one for those (whether Jew or Gentile) who embrace Jesus as Messiah. The latter comprise the church. The former are Jews who need not believe that Jesus is the Messiah but who relate savingly to God via Judaism and the covenant God uniquely established with them as a nation.

The correct view, in my opinion, is that there is only one new covenant. The church, being the historical continuation of the believing remnant within Israel, is the recipient of its blessings. Thus, both believing Jews and believing Gentiles, the latter of whom have been graciously included in the covenants of promise (Eph. 2:12), together and equally enjoy the fulfillment of all aspects of the new covenant (see esp. Matt. 26:28; Mark 14:24; Luke 22:20; 1 Cor. 11:25; 2 Cor. 3:6; Gal. 3:29; Eph. 2:11–22; 3:6; Heb. 8:6–13; 9:15; 10:15; 10:19ff.).

It is as a minister of this new covenant that Paul happily declares he has been made adequate or sufficient *by God*. He finds nothing in himself that would qualify him for this awesome task. God made him "competent" (2 Cor. 3:6), as is surely the case with each of us in the exercise of any spiritual gift or ministry or act of service to which God has called us.

What a blessing indeed that the superior glory of the "ministry of the Spirit" (v. 8) or the "ministry of righteousness" (v. 9), that is, the ministry of the new covenant, will never fade away or be abolished or replaced by one that surpasses it in power or preeminence (v. 11). For its provisions we give thanks, and on its power we rely as we seek to live to the glory of its Giver.

17

Bumped along the Pathway to Glory

2 Corinthians 3:18

And we all, with unveiled face, beholding the glory of the Lord, are being transformed into the same image from one degree of glory to another. For this comes from the Lord who is the Spirit.

There are times when I worry if I'm making progress in the Christian life. Honestly, there are times when I'm quite sure I'm not. I'm not talking about overt backsliding or moral regression, but a feeling of spiritual inertia that causes me to wonder if I'm moving forward toward greater conformity to Christ.

Of course, if I weren't making progress, I probably wouldn't be worried about whether I am or not! In other words, I take comfort from the fact that I'm *bothered* (the more spiritual word is "convicted") about those seasons when I don't seem to be living as I ought. It angers me not to see or sense an increase in holiness. There's a sense in which that itself *is* holiness, or at least the presence of a longing for it and a keen awareness of how far short I am of the righteousness of God.

I say all this as a way of highlighting the encouragement that is found in 2 Corinthians 3:18. For here I'm reassured that I'm not standing still, that the Spirit is at work within me, if only, at times, in small and often imperceptible ways. In the inner core of every Christian, in the depths of the heart, there is movement, as Paul says, "from one degree of glory to another" (v. 18). Literally, he writes that we are being transformed "*from* glory *unto* glory." The preposition "from" points to the *source* and "unto" highlights the ultimate *goal* in view. In other words, God began a work of grace in us at regeneration or the new birth that consisted of the experience of his glory that is building momentum and progressively moving toward the final experience of the fullness of that glory at the return of Jesus Christ. The ultimate glory in view here is described in other texts as well:

> But our citizenship is in heaven, and from it we await a Savior, the Lord Jesus Christ, who will *transform our lowly body to be like his glorious body*, by the power that enables him even to subject all things to himself. (Phil. 3:20–21)

> When Christ who is your life appears, then *you also will appear with him in glory.* (Col. 3:4)

> Beloved, we are God's children now, and what we will be has not yet appeared; but we know that *when he appears we shall be like him, because we shall see him as he is.* (1 John 3:2; cf. 1 Thess. 5:23)

Murray Harris put it best when he described this phenomenon as "a body suffused with the divine glory and perfectly adapted to the ecology of heaven."[1] I like that! But there's so much more in this passage that must be noted.

First, Paul describes us, *all Christians*, as those who are "beholding the glory of the Lord" and doing so, unlike the Israelites of old, "with unveiled face." It was the distinct privilege of Moses alone to glimpse the glory of God when he saw his "form" (Num. 12:8) and his "back" (Ex. 33:23). But now in the new covenant every Christian is privileged to behold that glory. And unlike the people of Israel who looked upon the glory as reflected in Moses' veiled face, we see with permanently uncovered faces.

Second, Paul's language suggests that we see the "glory of the Lord" indirectly, "mirrored," as it were, in "the face of Jesus" who is "the image of God." But where exactly do we "see" or "behold" that glory? Paul saw the glory of God on the road to Damascus (see Acts 22:11: "the brightness [lit., "glory"] of that light"; see also Acts 26:13). In 2 Corinthians 4:3–6 he suggests that God shines the glory of that light "in our hearts" through "the gospel." Thus as Barnett explains, "paradoxically, therefore, Paul's readers *see* the glory of Christ as they *hear* the gospel, which in turn gives the knowledge of God."[2]

It is important to point out that Paul does not suggest that we see the glory of Christ indistinctly or in a distorted way, but indirectly, "as over against our eschatologically seeing him 'face to face.' The imagery, therefore, is something quite positive, and it worked for Paul precisely because it allowed him to postulate a real 'seeing,' yet one that in the present age falls short of actually seeing the Lord 'face to face' as it were."[3] Or again, the apostle's point is that although our vision of this glory is mediated, it is inescapably clear, because the person of Christ who is revealed in the gospel is the exact and altogether perfect representation of God.

Third, the process that we call sanctification comes only as or because we behold the glory of God. Apart from beholding there is no becoming. The more we know him and behold him (see Ps. 27:4) in the splendor of his glory, the more we are changed into the very image of Jesus himself, in whose face God's glory has shined or is reflected (2 Cor. 4:4, 6). Sanctification, therefore, is the fruit of seeing and savoring. Ignorance, on the other hand, breeds moral paralysis (if not regression).

Fourth, Paul is clearly talking about the transformation of the *inner* person. "When Jesus was transfigured, the change was outwardly visible (Matt. 17:2), but when Christians are transformed, the change is essentially inward, the renewing of the mind (Rom. 12:2), and becomes visible only in their Christ-like behavior."[4] Of course, as we saw in several previous texts, the inner change will consummate in an outward transformation at the time of Christ's return. Until then, as Paul says later in 2 Corinthians 4:16, "though our outer self is wasting away, our inner self is being renewed day by day."

Fifth, as much as we all might wish otherwise, sanctification is progressive, not instantaneous. As noted earlier, we are gradually moving by the power of the Spirit from one stage or degree of glory (first "seen" in the gospel when we turn to Christ) to another (that of the glorified Jesus, whose glory we will not only see on the day of Christ's return but in which we will also participate).

Sixth, sanctification is by grace (we "*are being* transformed"), the agent of which is the Spirit of Christ. This doesn't eliminate human effort, but rather makes it possible. We act because we are acted upon. We work out our salvation with fear and trembling because God, who is always antecedent, is at work in us to will and to do for his good pleasure (see Phil. 2:12–13).

Seventh, and finally, we see here that "beholding is a way of becoming."[5] That is to say, we always tend to become like or take on the characteristics and qualities of whatever it is we admire and enjoy and cherish most. Fixing the eyes of our faith on Jesus is transformative. Gazing on his glory as seen in the gospel and now preserved for us in Scripture has the power to bump us along, as it were, whether minimally or maximally, whether in short spurts of sanctification or great and notable triumphs, toward the fullness that is found in Christ alone but will one day be found in us, by grace, as well!

So, be encouraged! Be strengthened! Be reassured! For "he who began a good work in you ['from glory'] will bring it to completion ['unto glory'] at the day of Jesus Christ" (Phil. 1:6).

Fighting Discouragement

2 Corinthians 4:1

Therefore, having this ministry by the mercy of God, we do not lose heart.

How do you fight discouragement? Or do you? Are you among those who simply yield to its relentless onslaught and give up?

People who fall into the latter category typically deal with disappointment in one of two ways. Some continue to work and "minister" (if that word is even appropriate to describe what they do) but do so with murmuring and impatience, bitterness toward God, self-pity within, and anger at anything that moves.

Others respond to the pain of disillusionment by anesthetizing their souls with sex, alcohol, or some other form of sensual self-indulgence, and then justify their actions by pointing to how poorly they've been treated (whether by God or people in the church or others from whom they're convinced they deserved better).

If anyone had a "right" to be discouraged, it might appear to be Paul. When one thinks of what he endured in the course of his life and ministry, he seems to be the perfect candidate for a "victim mentality" and the countless ways people use that attitude to rationalize sinful behavior. Yet, here in 2 Corinthians 4:1 he happily declares, "we do not lose heart!"

I can almost hear some say, "Well, for heaven's sake, I wouldn't lose heart either if I had Paul's gifts and eloquence and insights into the truth of God. And if I had been translated into the third heaven (2 Cor. 12:1–10) and seen great and glorious things, I could probably hang in there like he did." It's true, of course, that Paul was uniquely gifted by God and had been the recipient of numerous supernatural encounters. But that's not what kept him going. That's not what accounted for his ability to resist the temptation to throw in the towel.

To understand and account for his refusal to "lose heart" we need to look at verse 1 in its entirety: "Therefore, *having this ministry by the mercy of God*, we do not lose heart." There are actually two reasons Paul gives for why he overcame discouragement. They are related, yet distinct.

First, Paul had been entrusted with "this ministry," a reference to the ministry of the new covenant in the power of the Holy Spirit (described in chap. 3). Had he been called and commissioned to a ministry devoid of the Spirit's presence, I doubt he would have persevered as he did. Had "this ministry" been one characterized by legalism, a "ministry" energized by human effort rather than the power of the Spirit, Paul's response to persecution, slander, and imprisonment may well have been different.

What sustained him, at least in part, was the fact that he proclaimed a message of grace and the assurance of the Spirit's sanctifying presence (2 Cor. 3:18). Had he thought that those who embraced Christ as Lord would be left to themselves, dependent on their own resources, confronted by an external code of conduct without the guarantee of inward enablement, I doubt we'd be looking to him now as a model of maturity and a paradigm of perseverance!

But there's another reason why Paul did not lose heart or succumb to the otherwise natural human tendency to seek out safety and ease and opulence: Paul, like you and me, was a recipient of mercy. He certainly didn't deserve to be the minister of a gospel of grace or a covenant of divine power and promise. Paul, again like you and me, "was a privileged participant in the ministry of the new covenant purely on account of God's gratuitous favor" or mercy.[1]

The phrase translated "by the mercy of God" is similar in force to Paul's statement in Romans 11:31 where he speaks of "mercy shown." The verb in the original text (*eleethemen*) is what commentators call a "divine" or "theological passive" and could be rendered, "we were shown mercy (*by God*)." Neither Paul's calling as an apostle nor his competency to serve in that role nor his conversion by which he came to Christ had anything to do with his own efforts or initiative or resources. They were simply and solely and sufficiently the fruit of having been made the object of divine mercy.

Undoubtedly Paul was encouraged and upheld by reflecting on the *nature* of the new covenant ministry. But even more important still was his awareness that he was a participant in it and a minister to others of it, solely by God's sovereign kindness, compassion, and mercy. If you should ever think that your position in the kingdom of God is a reward rather than a gift, there will be little to sustain you in seasons of hardship and anguish. Only so far as you confess that although you deserved eternal death you instead received eternal life will you find power to persevere.

But how is it, precisely, that embracing divine mercy as the sole source of all you are and do, like Paul did, is a remedy for discouragement? The answer is that sovereign, saving mercy is incompatible not only with boasting but also with bitterness.

Consider Paul's challenge to the Corinthians in his first letter: "What do you have that you did not receive? If then you received it, why do you boast as if you did not receive it?" (1 Cor. 4:7). This is simply another way of saying, "Did you not receive everything by mercy rather than merit? OK, then act like it!" Knowing the truth of this text will turn your life inside out and upside down. The reality of sovereign, saving mercy transforms your view of both success and failure, both praise and persecution, both triumph and tragedy.

If your life and labors are, as Paul indicates, "by the mercy of God," you can neither take credit for what you've achieved nor complain about how you've been treated. All credit goes to God for the good and all blame to yourself for the bad.

One of my spiritual mentors, Russ McKnight, who is now with the Lord, would always respond to the question, "How are you doing?" with the answer, "Better than I deserve!" He wasn't trying to be cute, but he recognized that whatever benefits or blessings might come his way were not the payment of a debt but flowed from the fountain of divine mercy.

Paul said much the same thing in 1 Corinthians 15:10: "But by the grace of God I am what I am. . . ." If pressed to elaborate, I suspect he might have said:

"Yes, people have betrayed me, but I never deserved friends in the first place."

"Yes, many have slandered me, but I have no right to be well spoken of."

"I was the chief of sinners, but I was shown kindness! I deserved hell, but I got mercy!"

"How can I feel sorry for myself? Justice demanded my death, but I received life."

"How can I resent another's success when I never deserved any myself?"

Clearly, Paul's understanding of the role of mercy was the sustaining power in his soul that left no room for discouragement and gave no quarter to bitterness: "How can I possibly 'lose heart' when I deserved neither life nor breath nor opportunity nor eloquence nor a positive response on the part of those to whom I minister?"

Do you see your life in the same terms that Paul understood the ministry entrusted to him? What about your family? Your career? Perhaps the effective use of some spiritual gift or your status in the church? Are you in good health? Are your finances stable, even flourishing? What of the praise of your peers?

Can you look at everything in your life and honestly say, "It was by the mercy of God"? If not, you are a likely candidate either for arrogant boasting or for discouragement and the disheartening frustration that breeds bitterness and resentment. *Mercy is medicine for the discouraged soul.* The recommended dosage is daily.

Tampering with God's Word

2 Corinthians 4:2

But we have renounced disgraceful, underhanded ways. We refuse to practice cunning or to tamper with God's word, but by the open statement of the truth we would commend ourselves to everyone's conscience in the sight of God.

Earlier, in 2 Corinthians 3:17, the apostle Paul spoke of those who were "peddlers of God's word." In our meditation on that passage, I explained that he had in mind people who dilute the full strength of the gospel, perhaps eliminating (or at least minimizing) its offensive elements or altering certain theological points, so that the finished "product" will be more appealing to the audience. Their aim is to gain as large a following as possible, and especially the money that comes with it.

In 2 Corinthians 4:2 Paul returns to that theme, but with a slightly different emphasis. Here he declares that he refuses "to *tamper* with God's word," but instead is committed to "the open statement of the truth." Whereas in 3:17 the motivation appears to be monetary gain, in 4:2 the agenda is unclear. Certainly money may still be in view, but other factors ought also to be considered.

People often tamper with God's Word either to retain or expand their power base, to increase their popularity, or to avoid controversy and the discomfort it often creates. Some do so because of personal distaste for the hard truths of Scripture, to protect themselves against the contempt of those whose respect and acceptance they cherish, or in the interests of any number of personal agendas that require God's truth be treated as malleable and merely a means that may be manipulated to achieve whatever end is in view.

A brief glance across the broad spectrum of professing Christendom, if only here in America, reveals several expressions of the sort of tampering that Paul might well have in view.

One of the more explicit examples is the increasing trend toward either marginalizing or rejecting altogether the doctrine of penal substitutionary atonement. The unadulterated, sharp edge of the message of the cross in which Jesus Christ has, in our stead, propitiated the wrath of a holy God is more than some people can swallow. Such folk often insist they haven't rejected penal substitution but wish only to recast it in such a way that its unsavory elements are discarded lest we give unnecessary offence to a society that longs for a more compassionate and less "violent" Christianity. Others argue that they still embrace penal substitution but have simply repositioned it to a subordinate, tangential role in our understanding of atonement. In other words, penal substitution isn't altogether denied, it is simply dethroned from its formative status as the dominant and controlling model for what Christ accomplished and relegated to "one of many valid metaphors" for the sake of maintaining a more "holistic" view of Christ's saving work. Once this is done, the notion of penal substitution is, for all practical purposes, never heard from again.

In the final analysis, few if any of these efforts to redefine the doctrine of atonement can escape the charge of having tampered with God's Word. Many contend that they've merely *adapted* the gospel to a postmodern world but have stopped short of tampering with the truths of Scripture itself. I'll leave it for you to judge if that's true.

Another example of tampering with the text is the tendency to disregard certain teachings because of the difficulty they pose for life in the twenty-first century. I'm thinking particularly of the explosive growth among evangelicals of egalitarianism and the repudiation of any distinctions in role or responsibility between male and female, whether in marriage or ministry.

Again, of course, those who have yielded to this temptation would never countenance my use of the word "disregard." They would consider that an unfair, inflammatory, and pejorative assessment of what they've done. They insist that a new hermeneutical paradigm or model for reading Scripture has emerged that enables them to see that certain New Testament guidelines or principles previously thought to be timeless and binding on the conscience of Christians everywhere were, in fact, culturally accommodated or merely part of a trajectory of truth that liberates us from the explicit boundaries of New Testament teaching and elevates the church into that "ultimate ethic" toward which the text is, allegedly, pointing.

I've found that in many cases it isn't that people find comple-mentarianism to be biblically deficient or lacking in exegetical consistency.[1] Rather, it makes them feel like "fundamentalists" and threatens their acceptance and status within the broader evangelical community, especially the academy. Not wanting to be perceived as obscurantist or theologically naïve or culturally out of step, they relish these new proposals that appear to undermine the tradi-tional "hierarchical" (their word) understanding of the relationship between male and female in home and church. Wanting to be seen as progressive and in touch with the cutting edge of contemporary scholarship, they abandon a complementarian view of men and women for an "easier" and "more palatable" perspective.

Another example of what I consider tampering with God's Word is the growth of what George Barna has called the revolution among professing evangelicals who now find active participation in local church life unappealing and, worse still, unnecessary.[2]

Then, of course, there are those who don't like being branded as narrow-minded and arrogant exclusivists when it comes to the issue of salvation. The redemptive work of Christ may well be necessary as the foundation for any possibility of eternal life, but conscious faith in him alone is being discarded in favor of an inclusivism that now recognizes saving power in all (or most) non-Christian religions. The next (and seemingly inevitable) step for many is salvific universalism. Hell exists only in this life and on this earth, but is denied its eternal and penal dimensions.

Much could also be said of those who've tampered with God's Word to justify in their own minds an embrace of homosexuality as a legitimate lifestyle and same sex marriage as a "right" that should be recognized in our society.

Perhaps the most egregious and destructive example of tampering with the text doesn't involve any one doctrinal issue but reflects a diminishing loss of confidence in the functional authority of Scripture and a failure to believe and act upon the life-changing power of God's Word.

I'm persuaded that this is why we see so little expository preaching in our pulpits today. Although they would be extremely reticent to admit it publicly, countless pastors simply no longer believe that the biblical text, accurately explained and passionately applied, has the power to build the church. Operating with a secular standard of what constitutes "success" and under pressure to facilitate church growth (in every sense of the term), they have resorted to gimmicks, props, marketing techniques, and entertainment to the obvious detriment, and all too frequent abandonment, of exposition.

This inevitably leads to a loss of the *functional* authority of Scripture in church life. Whereas most would be quick to affirm the inspiration of the Bible in their statements of faith, few actually bend their beliefs to conform to Scripture or subordinate their personal preferences to the principles of the text. Affirmation of biblical authority is all too often *only* affirmation, with little effort made to actually yield or submit to the dictates of what God has revealed.

An illustration of this latter point is found in a national survey conducted by Christianity Today International and Zondervan publishers, the results of which appeared in *Leadership* magazine. To cite only one example, a man named James Smith identified himself as a Christian, but said that he does not necessarily believe that his God is any different from the one his Muslim friend worships. "I don't think that God would be a God who would shut others out of heaven because they don't use the word 'Christian' to describe themselves," said Smith.[3]

With all due respect, and allowing that I may have misinterpreted his comments, it doesn't matter what Smith thinks. Christians are not free to retain what they want to be true and spurn the clear teaching of Scripture. If Scripture is inspired, it is authoritative. And if it is authoritative, we must bow to its principles and truths even when they are uncomfortable, unpopular, or put a strain between us and friends who may believe otherwise. We dare not tamper with God's Word. Ever.

Whatever our calling in life, whatever our career or ministry, my prayer is that we would say with Paul: "We have renounced disgraceful, underhanded ways. We refuse to practice cunning or to tamper with God's word, but by the open statement of the truth we would commend ourselves to everyone's conscience in the sight of God" (2 Cor. 4:2).

The Gospel: Veiled and Unveiled

2 Corinthians 4:3–4

And even if our gospel is veiled, it is veiled only to those who are perishing. In their case the god of this world has blinded the minds of the unbelievers, to keep them from seeing the light of the gospel of the glory of Christ, who is the image of God.

If you want to maintain a reputation in secular society for being culturally sophisticated, educated, and enlightened, don't ever mention the fact that you believe in a literal devil. Few things will more quickly and thoroughly sabotage your reputation and standing than letting it be known that you believe demonic spirits are real and active and to an extent are responsible for why those who are mocking you are, in fact, mocking you.

On the other hand, if you are more concerned about being true to the Word of God than you are about retaining the respect of the enemies of Christ, there are a few biblical texts that demand our attention.

What makes these passages so remarkable is that they portray unbelievers as being in the grip of an alien power, in bondage to and blinded by none other than Satan himself. I say this is remarkable because the one thing on which most non-Christians pride themselves is their alleged freedom or autonomy and their enlightened perspective on life.

The apostle Paul would beg to differ. In Ephesians 2:2, he declares that all the unregenerate and unbelieving (and that included you before your conversion) follow "the prince of the power of the air, the spirit that is now at work in the sons of disobedience." Satan is at "work" (*energeo*) in the unbeliever, a word used earlier in Ephesians of God's activity in the world (1:11) in general and in the resurrection of Jesus in particular (1:20). This does *not* mean that all unbelievers are demon possessed, but refers to Satan's supernatural activity by which he exerts a negative influence over the lives of those who reject Jesus.

If that isn't explicit enough for you, consider John's startling declaration that whereas Christians are "from God" and "in" Christ (1 John 5:19–20), "the whole world lies in the power of the evil one" (1 John 5:19).

The point is that everyone is in someone! "John wastes no words and blurs no issues. The uncompromising alternative is stated baldly. Everyone belongs either to 'us' or to the 'world.' Everyone is therefore either 'of God' or 'in the evil one.' There is no third category."[1]

This forever shatters the illusion of *neutrality*, the idea that so-called "good" people who are not Christians are neither for God nor for Satan, are neither in God's kingdom nor in Satan's. The fact is, all people, young and old, male and female, belong to one of two kingdoms: the kingdom of light or the kingdom of darkness. If one is not "in Christ" one is "in the power of the evil one," even if there is no visible, sensible awareness of being in the devil's grip. Thus, *not to serve God is to serve Satan* whether one is conscious of it or not.

Finally, consider our text in 2 Corinthians 4:3–4 where Paul accounts for human unbelief by declaring that "if our gospel is veiled, it is veiled only to those who are perishing. In their case the god of this world has blinded the minds of the unbelievers, to keep them from seeing the light of the gospel of the glory of Christ, who is the image of God."

Some in the Corinthian church may have suggested that wide-spread unbelief and callous rejection of the gospel invalidates its claim to truth. Perhaps some argued that the spurning of the light of the gospel casts a shadow on its luster. But the glory of the good news does not guarantee its acceptance. "The blindness of unbelievers," John Calvin said, "in no way detracts from the clearness of the gospel, for the sun is no less resplendent because the blind do not perceive its light."[2]

Paul's adversaries would have pointed to opposition to his message as a way of casting aspersions on his apostolic calling and to undermine his authority in the Corinthian church. Of course Paul was well aware that notwithstanding his determination to be free of deception, and the clarity, boldness, and sincerity with which he preached, many rejected the message of the cross. But the reason for this veiling wasn't some failure in Paul's character or an inherent defect in the gospel itself but rather a conjunction of two forces: the unbelief of those who are perishing and Satan's activity in blinding them.

Earlier in 2 Corinthians 3:14–16 the "veiling" lay over the hearts of Jews when the writings of Moses were read, whereas here the veil remains on the minds of unbelievers when the gospel is preached. The problem isn't that they don't understand what the gospel means, as if it were illogical or incoherent. Nor does Paul mean that they lacked the necessary faculties of mind and will to embrace Christ in faith. Their refusal to believe is due to a *hatred* of both God and the gospel. They find nothing in him or it attractive or appealing or worthwhile. Their treasure is the world, and they see nothing in Christ crucified that would lead them to believe he is worthy of their affection and devotion.

Be it also noted that the "unbelievers" (v. 4) whom Paul describes are not simply lacking faith in Christ. They are actively antagonistic toward him. Their hearts seethe with hostility (see Rom. 3:10–18). It isn't the case that they are indifferent or disinterested, far less that they want to believe in Christ but Satan intervenes and prevents it. They are already refusing to believe, choosing to put their hope and trust in anything other than Jesus. Satan doesn't blind the minds of otherwise "good" people, compelling them against their will to become unbelievers. Rather he blinds or aggravates the hardness of heart in which they revel and delight.

Scott Hafemann, on the other hand, insists that "people are not blinded because they choose to renounce the gospel, rather, they choose to renounce the gospel because they are blind. And they are not blind because they choose to be so, but because Satan has made them so."[3] But the text indicates that those in whom Satan is operative and on whom blindness is inflicted are already in unbelief. Satan's role is to compound the hopelessness of the unbeliever by aggravating and intensifying a resistance to the truth that is already festering in their souls.

What they do not see is the light that comes or flows from the gospel that embodies or contains the glory of Christ Jesus. Consider the nature of defective eyesight and how this can be used to understand why people cannot see the glory of God in the gospel.

Some suffer physically from myopia or nearsightedness. Likewise, some suffer in the same way spiritually because they cannot see beyond themselves and their own selfish interests.

Some suffer physically from hyperopia or farsightedness. Likewise, some suffer in the same way spiritually because they can only see the world and its glitter and not the need of their own heart.

Still others suffer physically from presbyopia or inelasticity of the lens that comes from old age. Likewise, some suffer in the same way spiritually because they have grown old looking at the gospel and, with the passing of time, decay and spiritual petrifaction have set in.

Is there, then, no hope for a lost and dying world? Indeed, there is! But it requires an act of sovereign, saving mercy in which the God who spoke light into the primeval darkness (Genesis 1) yet again shines in the hearts of men and women to give them "the light of the knowledge of the glory of God in the face of Jesus Christ" (2 Cor. 4:6).

Satan is indeed active and operative and powerful in his efforts to blind and bind those who know not Christ. But God's gracious work through his Spirit is more powerful still. Our prayer for unsaved friends and family must be that God would sovereignly dispel the darkness of unbelief and shine the light of truth into their hardened and spiritually lifeless souls, giving them a taste for the sweetness of the saving mercies of Christ and an eye for his incomparable beauty.

A Divine and Supernatural Light

2 Corinthians 4:5–6

For what we proclaim is not ourselves, but Jesus Christ as Lord, with ourselves as your servants for Jesus' sake. For God, who said, "Let light shine out of darkness," has shone in our hearts to give the light of the knowledge of the glory of God in the face of Jesus Christ.

If Satan is actively blinding the minds of unbelievers to compound and perpetuate their bondage in spiritual darkness (2 Cor. 4:3–4), what possible hope is there? We seem left only to despair of unsaved loved ones. What, if anything, can bring the unregenerate into life? What, if anything, can dispel the darkness of unbelief and awaken the heart to the beauty of Christ? What, if anything, can we do in the face of such satanic opposition?

The answer, Paul said, is to proclaim the gospel that Jesus Christ is Lord (2 Cor. 4:5)! Through the gospel, and only the gospel, is the light that brings life to be found.

In August of 1734, Jonathan Edwards (1703–1758) preached one of his most famous sermons, rather cumbersomely titled *A Divine and Supernatural Light, Immediately Imparted to the Soul by the Spirit of God, Shown to Be Both Scriptural and Rational Doctrine.* In this sermon, among other things, he explained the essence of the saving experience. What is it, precisely, that occurs when God causes new life to erupt from within the depths of a spiritual corpse?

The apostle Paul's answer is that "God, who said, 'Let light shine out of darkness, [shines] in our hearts to give the light of the knowledge of the glory of God in the face of Jesus Christ" (2 Cor. 4:6). "You cannot go beneath this," John Piper says. "There is no deeper reality and no greater value than the glory of God in Christ. There is no prize and no satisfaction beyond this. When you have this, you are at the end. You are home. The glory of God is not a means to anything greater. This is ultimate, absolute reality. All true salvation ends here, not before and not beyond. There is no beyond. The glory of God in Christ is what makes the gospel *gospel.*"[1]

Seeing this light and knowing this knowledge and relishing the beauty of God's glory as revealed in the face of Jesus Christ are utterly impossible for fallen and depraved people unless God sovereignly shines his regenerating and saving mercy into our hearts, thereby dispelling the darkness of unbelief and hostility and bringing to us a new sense of the sweetness and majesty of Jesus.

The contrast between 2 Corinthians 4:6 and 4:4 is shocking. Unbelievers are blinded by Satan. Believers are enlightened by God. Satan takes one from unbelief into total darkness. God takes one from total darkness into the brilliance of Christ's light!

The obvious background for Paul's language is Genesis 1:2–3 (cf. Acts 26:12–18). The original, primeval darkness that enshrouded the creation was dispelled by the divinely creative command: "Let there be light!" Likewise, by way of analogy, in sovereign, creative mercy, God fixes his gaze upon the darkness of sin, death, and blindness in the human soul and says, "Let there be light!"

We must not miss the emphasis Paul places on the glory of the gospel as it is proclaimed and what it means to those who believe. Paul himself literally saw the glory of God revealed in the literal face of Jesus when he was on the Damascus road. That which Paul saw, he now sets forth by means of "the truth" (v. 2) of the gospel addressed to the ears of his hearers (i.e., to the Corinthians, to you and me).

When we by grace respond in faith, light from the glorified Christ shines into our darkened hearts (v. 6). As Paul Barnett points out, "such 'seeing' of 'the light . . . of the glory' is, of course, metaphorical for *hearing*. The gospel of Christ comes first not as an optical but as an aural reality (see Rom. 10:17; Gal. 3:2, 5; cf. 3:1). Nonetheless, his words are not merely figurative. The intensity of Paul's language suggests that he is appealing to shared spiritual experience, his own and his readers'. When the gospel is heard and the hearer turns to the Lord, the veil is removed so that he now 'sees' the glory of the Lord (see on 3:16, 18)."[2]

Don't miss this: *the glory of God is present in the proclamation of the gospel* (4:4–6)! This is why Paul is so offended by the "peddlers of God's word" (2:17) in Corinth and those who "tamper with" the gospel (4:2). This is not a matter of mere words or a routine speech or a competitive attempt to appear more powerful or persuasive or verbally impressive than the other guy.

The proclamation of the truth of the gospel is not entertainment. It is not a platform for a preacher to enhance his reputation or pad his pocketbook or impress people with his eloquence. A preacher or teacher must never open the Scriptures flippantly or casually, as if setting forth the truths of the gospel were no different from any other form of communication.

The same applies anytime anyone shares the gospel with a passing stranger in a restaurant or distributes a tract to a friend. Just think of it: when you speak or write or share the message of the cross, "the light of the knowledge of the glory of God [as revealed] in the face of Jesus" (v. 6) is shining forth. What an awesome calling we have! What an exquisite treasure we carry (4:7)!

Edwards referred to this phenomenon as the shining forth of a divine and supernatural light. This experience, he argued, is not to be identified with the conviction of sin that unregenerate people experience. The Spirit can act upon the soul of an unbeliever without communicating himself to or uniting himself with that person. Nor is it to be identified with "impressions" made upon the "imagination." It has nothing to do with seeing anything with one's physical eyes.

The divine and supernatural light, said Edwards, does not suggest or impart new truths or ideas not already found in the written Word of God. It "only gives a due apprehension of those things that are taught in the Word of God."[3]

We must also be careful not to identify it with those occasions when the unregenerate are deeply and profoundly affected by religious ideas. One may be moved or stirred or emotionally impacted by a religious phenomenon without believing it to be true (consider, for example, the widespread popular reaction to Mel Gibson's film, *The Passion*).

So what is this "divine and supernatural light" that Paul describes in 2 Corinthians 4:6? Edwards defined it as "a true sense [or "apprehension"] of the divine excellency of the things revealed in the Word of God, and a conviction of the truth and reality of them, thence arising."[4] This is a profoundly supernatural experience in which a person doesn't "merely rationally believe that God is glorious, but . . . has a sense of the gloriousness of God in his heart."[5]

If you are wondering what the difference is between "rationally" believing that God is glorious and having a "sense of the excellency" of God's glory, it is the difference between knowing that God is holy and having a "sense of the loveliness" of God's holiness. It is not only a "speculatively judging that God is gracious" but also "a sense [of] how amiable God is upon that account" or sensing the "beauty" of God's grace and holiness.

An unregenerate person may have a cognitive awareness or knowledge of the terms of the gospel of Christ. But to recognize and relish the beauty or amiableness or sweetness of that truth and feel pleasure and delight in it are due wholly to the regenerating work of the Spirit. As Edwards said, "there is a difference between having a rational judgment that honey is sweet, and having a sense of its sweetness."[6] In other words, "when the heart is sensible of the beauty and amiableness of a thing, *it necessarily feels pleasure in the apprehension*."[7]

How does God shine this light into our hearts? He first "destroys the enmity, removes those prejudices, and sanctifies the reason [of a person], and causes it to lie open to the force of arguments for their truth."[8] He also causes the gospel to be more lively and enables the mind to focus and think and concentrate with more intensity on what is known. But this divine and supernatural light also enables the mind and heart, by "a kind of intuitive and immediate evidence," to be convinced of the truth of the superlative excellency of what is proclaimed in the gospel of Christ as Lord. Said Edwards:

> Men have a great deal of pleasure in human knowledge, in studies of natural things; but this is nothing to that joy which arises from this divine light shining into the soul. This light gives a view of those things that are immensely the most exquisitely beautiful, and capable of delighting the eye of the understanding. This spiritual light is the dawning of the light of glory in the heart.[9]

It's hard to put into words the enjoyment, delight, and sense of the sweetness of God that the Spirit imparts to the soul of man! Peter calls it "joy that is inexpressible and filled with glory" (1 Pet. 1:8). What a marvelous blessing, indeed, with which nothing else in heaven or earth can compare, that hell-deserving sinners have imparted to them a "new sense of the heart" that consists in delight and enjoyment and an intuitive awareness or apprehension of the sweetness of God's beauty as revealed in the face of Jesus Christ.

Let us by all means "praise God from whom all blessings flow," and in doing so remember that this, dear friend, is the greatest blessing of all.

22

Jars of Clay and the Glory of God

2 Corinthians 4:7

But we have this treasure in jars of clay, to show that the surpassing power belongs to God and not to us.

A ll of us at one time or another, and some more than others, fear that our weakness is a barrier to God's purposes. We feel so very keenly the promptings of our flesh, the lack of emotional energy, our ignorance of basic truths, not to mention physical exhaustion or sickness, anxiety, and self-doubt. Then, of course, there is the absence of political and social influence, the ridicule incurred for following Christ and, for some, oppression and more severe forms of persecution and suffering.

It's so easy to fall into the trap of thinking that if God wants to accomplish something of greatness he needs great people to do it. We think he needs, and will choose, people with power, personality, charisma, money; people who are physically impressive and verbally eloquent; people whose names appear regularly in newspapers or on blogs; people whose lives seem to make a significant impact on our culture; people that history will remember with fondness and appreciation.

I'm not suggesting that such people are of no use to God or that their earthly achievements can't be redeemed for the sake of the kingdom. But they do have one distinct disadvantage (that's right, *dis*advantage). They are far more prone to take for themselves credit that belongs to God. Weak people apologize far more than they boast. Strong people, beautiful people, people with money and status, are more inclined to draw attention to themselves and divert praise from the One to whom alone all glory is due.

Make no mistake about it, God is determined to secure all the glory for himself! I hope you're OK with that, for your ultimate joy is dependent on God being God. Were God to be less than supremely glorious and praiseworthy, we are the ones who stand to lose. Our ultimate and eternal satisfaction is dependent on his being ultimately and eternally satisfying. If God should ever be less than infinitely deserving of all praise and honor and credit for whatever good is achieved, our delight in him is to that extent diminished. His capacity to enthrall us is to that extent undermined. A God who gets only partial credit is a God who is worthy of only partial praise, and such a "god" would hardly warrant our adoration or be capable of eliciting, much less sustaining, our eternal enjoyment.

This alone makes sense of Paul's statement in 2 Corinthians 4:7: "But we have this treasure in jars of clay, to show that the surpassing power belongs to God and not to us." If any degree of power derives from us, or if the praise it deserves should go to someone or something other than God, to that degree we endure irrevocable loss.

This is why Paul was so unaffected and undisturbed by his obvious weaknesses. He was keenly aware of his shortcomings, his lack of eloquence, and his physical frailty. "If I must boast," Paul said in 2 Corinthians 11:30, "I will boast of the things that show my weakness." He had in mind such things as "greater labors, far more imprisonments, . . . countless beatings" and near death experiences (2 Cor. 11:23). Add to that being "beaten with rods," being stoned, suffering shipwreck, and being in constant danger from thieves and both Jew and Gentile, not to mention what he encountered while on the sea or in the wilderness (2 Cor. 11:24–26). Then there were times of toil and hardship and sleepless nights, even hunger and thirst and cold and exposure (2 Cor. 11:27).

These aren't typically the sorts of things we associate with greatness. It's not likely that such a person would evoke much praise or attain to great heights of earthly prominence. And that's fine with Paul, because it meant that whatever might be accomplished through him would redound to the glory of God alone. This is why he would "not venture to speak of anything except what Christ has accomplished . . ." through him (Rom. 15:18).

It's hard to envision anything more glorious or inherently majestic than the gospel that Paul has just described in 2 Corinthians 4:5–6, a gospel that embodies and expresses the radiant splendor and glory of God as revealed in the face of Jesus Christ. But lest anyone think that Paul had a hand in its creation or was in any way or to any degree responsible for the marvelous, Christ-exalting, life-giving, soul-cleansing, sin-killing effects it produces, he is quick to declare that God has entrusted this indescribable "treasure" to "jars of clay" like himself.

As Philip Hughes has said,

> There could be no contrast more striking than that between the greatness of the divine glory and the frailty and unworthiness of the vessels in which it dwells and through which it is manifested to the world. Paul's calumniators had contemptuously described his bodily appearance as weak and his speech as of no account (10:10; cf. 10:1; 11:6; 12:7), hoping thereby to discredit his authority. But it is one of the main purposes of this epistle to show that this immense discrepancy between the treasure and the vessel serves simply to attest that human weakness presents no barrier to the purposes of God, indeed, that God's power is made perfect in weakness (12:9), as the brilliance of a treasure is enhanced and magnified by comparison with a common container in which it is placed.[1]

The unmistakable, inescapable design behind this incredible contrast between the splendor of the treasure and the earthiness of the vessel is so that the surplus or excess or exceeding abundance of the power may be seen to be wholly of God and not from any one of us. Indeed, contrary to the beliefs and expectations of the world, which thinks only in terms of human ability and accomplishment, "it is precisely the Christian's utter frailty which lays him open to the experience of the all-sufficiency of God's grace, so that he is able even to rejoice because of his weakness."[2]

If a treasure were deposited in a chest laden with gold and covered with precious jewels, people might focus on the container and ignore the contents. This accounts for why those who bring the greatest glory to God are often those who are least impressive when judged by human standards alone.

There would appear to be something of a tension in this truth. On the one hand, as Christians we must always strive for excellence. We must never think that being "jars of clay" requires mediocrity or a slipshod approach to life, far less that we slack off in our use of all the opportunities God has given us. Failing to employ every resource at our disposal or taking on any task or ministry carelessly or halfheartedly is never endorsed in God's Word.

On the other hand, we dare not ever think that what we achieve, we do so without God's help or energizing presence. We must never put forth ourselves as preeminent or in such a way that the glory of God is obscured or his sustaining grace is marginalized.

The weakness in view here is primarily reflected in our suffering for righteousness' sake. Although persecuted, Paul persevered. The former revealed his frailty, the latter God's strength. You may not be extraordinary (according to human standards), but God is.

Society often marginalizes believers in Jesus, and believers rarely gain access to the corridors of power. Their voices are muted, and their lives are oppressed. When judged by the standards of the world, the church appears insignificant and inconsequential. How can people who value humility above pride and self-sacrifice over ruthless ambition be taken seriously? Those who are called upon to love their enemies rather than kill them, to forsake vengeance, and to do good to those who hate them are especially vulnerable to mistreatment and disdain.

Yet these are the people perfectly positioned to ensure that whatever they achieve be credited to God. God has sovereignly orchestrated the salvation of the weak and despised, the foolish and the frail, so that when much is achieved, he, rather than they, will be honored.

Not everyone is willing to embrace this divine design. They resent being clay jars. They deserve better, or so they think. Faith, so-called, will deliver them from the weakness and finitude of being human. Ministry, so-called, is simply a tool for transforming the earthen pot into a priceless vase. Such folk do, undeniably, appear more powerful and appealing and successful. And God less so. That's a high price to pay.

23

Knocked Down, but Not Out

2 Corinthians 4:8–12

We are afflicted in every way, but not crushed; perplexed, but not driven to despair; persecuted, but not forsaken; struck down, but not destroyed; always carrying in the body the death of Jesus, so that the life of Jesus may also be manifested in our bodies. For we who live are always being given over to death for Jesus' sake, so that the life of Jesus also may be manifested in our mortal flesh. So death is at work in us, but life in you.

I recently spoke briefly with a longtime friend who is facing yet another round of intense treatments for a recurring brain tumor. The dosage level of pain medication that he requires simply to survive each day is almost incomprehensible. When I got off the phone, visibly shaken, my wife asked me how he was doing. It seemed only fitting to answer, "He's afflicted in every way, but not crushed; quite obviously he and his family are perplexed, but not driven to despair; I'm not sure if he feels persecuted, but I know he doesn't feel forsaken; he's certainly been struck down, but just as certainly not destroyed."

Given my current meditations on 2 Corinthians 4, this seemed the appropriate language to describe his situation. I can assure you

117

of this, there's not the slightest chance he'll be inclined to rely on his own strength or to point to himself as one deserving glory and honor. He is very much in touch with the reality of being a jar of clay (2 Cor. 4:7) to whom God has wisely entrusted the exquisite treasure of the revelation of the glory of Jesus Christ (2 Cor. 4:6).

It's striking to note how differently Christians react to suffering and hardship. The conclusions they draw about their source and design are shockingly at odds. In fact, I'm increasingly convinced that how one responds to trials and affliction is perhaps the most accurate monitor of our maturity in Christ. That being the case, I can't imagine a more mature and Christlike man than my friend.

Some, surprisingly, actually *deny* that such trials really exist. These people aren't optimistic; they are simply unrealistic, or perhaps they fear that to acknowledge weakness and hardship and turmoil would be an admission of sin or immaturity or, worst of all (to their way of thinking), a lack of faith.

Others fall into *despair* because of the overwhelming and seemingly inexplicable onset of suffering. They encounter something similar to what Paul endured and immediately conclude that God hates them or has abandoned them, so why bother trying.

Some insist such calamities are *demonic*. All such trials and tribulations, they argue, are from Satan, not God. Of course, Satan certainly has it in his heart (assuming he has a "heart") to torment and oppress God's people. Job immediately comes to mind. But in all such cases, Job included, no one lays a hand on God's people apart from either God's permission or his direct decree.

Finally, a few, like Paul, see them as *divinely* ordained, lovingly orchestrated opportunities for our growth, the salvation of others, and above all else, God's glory.

Second Corinthians 4:8–9 contains four antitheses designed to illustrate what Paul had in mind when he spoke of our being "jars of clay" in which God has deposited the gospel of the grace of God in Christ. A couple of things should be noted before we examine them.

The first experience noted in each pair is an illustration of human weakness, while the second illustrates divine strength. In each case Paul's point is that "to be at the end of man's resources is not to be at the end of God's resources; on the contrary, it is to be precisely in the position best suited to prove and benefit from them, and to experience the surplus of the power of God breaking through and resolving the human dilemma."[1]

Another feature to note is the *constant* nature of these afflictions, as seen both in the phrase "in every way" (perhaps better rendered "at all times") and the temporal adverbs in verse 10 (*pantote*) and verse 11 (*aei*), both of which are translated "always." Paul does not envision a time in this life when such suffering will diminish or disappear. Faithful Christians will always be subjected to such treatment. As Murray Harris has said, "so far from being an anomaly or a proof of the illegitimacy of his claim to apostleship (as some of his Corinthian opponents seemed to believe), his afflictions and hardships were the badge of his apostolicity, evidence that the power of God rested upon him."[2]

In other words, Paul does not have in mind some temporary phenomenon from which we live in hope of being delivered. This "dying" is daily. This spiritual "being delivered over to death" is as much a part of being a Christian as breathing is a part of physical living. To look at Paul was to see in process a dying analogous to that which Jesus experienced. Each time he was delivered, each time he overcame an obstacle, additional evidence was given that the crucified Jesus is also the resurrected Lord!

So let's look now at these four realities of Christian experience.

First, Paul was "afflicted in every way, but not crushed" (v. 8a). The word "afflicted" is a broad, all-encompassing term that includes physical, spiritual, and psychological oppression. Notwithstanding the multitude of ways in which this was manifest, Paul never felt "crushed" or so confined that he lost hope in God.

Second, he was "perplexed, but not driven to despair" (v. 8b), or as one commentator put it, "at a loss but not completely baffled."[3] Philip Hughes translates it, "confused but not confounded."[4] Though often with no explanation or answer that would account for what he endured, Paul never felt as if there were none. God always has a reason for permitting or even orchestrating such suffering, although we may have to wait until heaven to discover it.

Third, he was "persecuted, but not forsaken" (v. 9a). Surely Paul has in mind being persecuted by men but never abandoned by God. Man's abuse of us is no measure of God's affection!

The word translated "forsaken" is the one Jesus used in his cry of dereliction: "My God, my God, why have you *forsaken* me?" (Mark 15:34). Is Paul suggesting that although God actually did "forsake" Jesus on the cross, as he endured the punishment of our sin, he will never "forsake" us? Is not the former the reason for the latter?

Fourth, he was "struck down, but not destroyed" (v. 9b), or as someone once said, "knocked down, but not knocked out."

Each of these pairs of words is designed to illustrate as vividly as possible Paul's frailty as a "jar of clay" and his absolute dependence on the superlative excellence and abundant supply of God's power.

It's important to note the relationship between verses 10 and 11 and the antitheses of verses 8 and 9. That is to say, "the death of Jesus" in verse 10 and "being given over to death for Jesus' sake" in verse 11 together summarize what it means to be "afflicted," "perplexed," "persecuted," and "struck down." Likewise, "the life of Jesus" in verses 10 and 11 accounts for Paul's not being "crushed" or "driven to despair" or "forsaken" or "destroyed" while suffering.

The "life of Jesus" is "the deliverance represented by the four 'but nots' of those verses. The former (the 'dying of Jesus') were endured precisely in order that rescue from them (the 'life of Jesus') might be experienced."[5]

Note well that carrying about in himself the "death" of Jesus is simultaneous with the expression through him, for the sake of others, of the "life" of Jesus! The latter doesn't eliminate the former. On the contrary, it is only by Paul's experiencing life-threatening persecution and suffering that Christ's life-giving power is made available to the Corinthians (and to us). In other words, "the very purpose of the believer's identification with Jesus in his sufferings is to provide an opportunity for the display of Jesus' risen life."[6]

The phrase, we "are always being given over to death" (v. 11) is what we call a divine passive. In other words, we are always being given over to death *by God*! Paul's point is "that his sufferings are not merely coincidental, but part of the divine plan for the spread of the gospel."[7]

Thus, again, when Paul says in verse 12 that "death is at work in us," he has specifically in mind the experiences noted in the first half of the antitheses of verses 8–9, as well as verse 10 and 11. We should also ponder the paradox of asserting that "death" is "at work"! Death, by definition, is the absence of life and activity. Yet Paul says that the very "life" that has come to the Corinthians is the result of the "death" that works in him! By "death," of course, he has in mind again those sufferings in ministry described in verses 8–9.

And what of my friend? Why is he not crushed or driven to despair or forsaken or destroyed, though his body is ravaged by this life-threatening tumor? What accounts for his triumph in the midst of such obvious tragedy? There is only one answer: his undying (though admittedly shaken) faith in the sustaining power and superlative promise of eternal life through the grace of God as revealed in Jesus Christ.

Do I continue to pray for his healing? Yes, always. But whether he lives or dies, the resurrection life of Jesus is ever so vividly manifest through him to me.

24

Faith over Fear

2 Corinthians 4:13–15

Since we have the same spirit of faith according to what has been written, "I believed, and so I spoke," we also believe, and so we also speak, knowing that he who raised the Lord Jesus will raise us also with Jesus and bring us with you into his presence. For it is all for your sake, so that as grace extends to more and more people it may increase thanksgiving, to the glory of God.

Fear can be a paralyzing force in the life of the Christian. Whether from fear of being rejected or persecuted or perhaps not wanting to be seen as lacking cogent answers to controversial questions, many remain silent.

I doubt if there has ever been a believer who hasn't at some time kept his mouth shut when he should have spoken. With hindsight, we look back on the occasion and feel the sting of guilt, even shame, for having let cowardice rather than courage dictate our behavior.

Many of you are familiar with the famous incident at the Diet of Worms in 1521 when Martin Luther stood resolute and firm in affirming his faith. On April 17 Luther was challenged with two questions. First, did he acknowledge that the books on the table

122

before him were his? And second, would he stand by them or retract what he had written?

"Yes, the books are mine," Luther said. "But whether I shall reaffirm in the same terms all, or shall retract what I may have uttered beyond the authority of Scripture,—because the matter involves a question of faith and of the salvation of souls, and because it concerns the Word of God, which is the greatest thing in heaven and on earth, and which we all must reverence,—it would be dangerous and rash in me to make any unpremeditated declaration, because in unpremeditated speech I might say something less than the fact and something more than the truth; besides, I remember the saying of Christ when He declared, 'Whosoever shall deny Me before men, him will I also deny before My Father which is in heaven, and before His angels.' For these reasons I beg, with all respect, that your Imperial Majesty give me time to deliberate, that I may answer the question without injury to the Word of God and without peril to my own soul."

Returning on April 18, he delivered this now famous response:

Unless I am refuted and convicted by testimonies of the Scriptures or by clear arguments (since I believe neither the Pope nor councils alone; it being evident that they have often erred and contradicted themselves), I am conquered by the Holy Scriptures quoted by me, and my conscience is bound to the Word of God: I cannot and I will not recant anything, since it is unsafe and dangerous to do anything against the conscience. Here I stand. I cannot do otherwise. God help me. Amen!

Our circumstances are less threatening. It isn't with exile or death that we are threatened when challenged about our faith. Yet we long to speak with the same clarity and courage that Luther did. Is it possible? If so, how?

Paul was faced on countless occasions with a similar situation. Scorn, ridicule, imprisonment, beatings, and the possibility of martyrdom threatened him each time he ventured to open his mouth. Yet he refused to remain silent! How did he do it? How might we do it?

Here in 2 Corinthians 4:13–15 we catch a glimpse of what motivated and sustained Paul in his courageous and unflinching defense of the gospel. Five factors played a role in sustaining him in his bold witness for Christ.

First, boldness is buoyed by belief. "We also believe," Paul said, "and so we also speak." The Holy Spirit who first awakened faith in our hearts, Paul says, has produced in us a deep and abiding conviction of the truth of the gospel. In spite of the daily experience of "death" (vv. 10–12), Paul's unswerving confidence in God's purposes in Christ made it inevitable and inescapable that he should continue to preach. Belief in the truth has a remarkably powerful capacity to generate courage in the face of the enemy.

Second, Paul speaks in the face of all opposition because he knows "that he who raised the Lord Jesus will raise us also with Jesus." In other words, what ultimate harm can any man inflict on Paul if God has pledged himself to raise him up with Christ on the last day? Yes, they can crush the body, but God will glorify it. Yes, they can terminate his temporal existence, but God has promised eternal life. Undoubtedly Paul would have strengthened himself in moments of weakness and fear with the reminder: "The same God who raised Jesus from the dead will raise me from the dead. So let them kill me, if that is what it takes to make known the truth of the glory of God in Christ."

Third, courage to confront unbelief with the truth comes from knowing that God has pledged to "bring us . . . into his presence." The prospect of standing unashamed and joyful in the blinding, breathtaking presence of the glory of God was enough to sustain Paul and to energize his otherwise hesitant heart (see Jude 24).

Paul confessed his need for boldness and asked that other Christians pray for him in that regard (see Eph. 6:19). I suspect that when God answered that prayer, he did so, at least in part, by reminding the apostle that one day he would stand before him, never again to be insulted, never again to be afflicted, forever and again to be enthralled and captivated by God's ineffable beauty.

Fourth, Paul could hardly remain silent knowing that to speak boldly was for the sake of the Corinthians whom he loved so dearly. "For it is all for your sake," he said to them, "so that as grace extends to more and more people it may increase thanksgiving, to the glory of God." My ministry has you in view, Paul said. If I were to cease speaking, if I were to yield to intimidation or pressure or threat of persecution, you are the ones who would suffer loss, for the "grace" that comes through the gospel would not reach those who need it most.

Fifth, and finally, there is an even greater impulse at work in Paul's heart that accounts for his vocal bravery. As I speak, Paul said, the saving and sanctifying grace of God extends to more and more people. And as this grace is embraced and enjoyed, its recipients turn their hearts toward heaven with passionate and whole-souled gratitude to God. And when they do, *he is glorified!*

It should come as no surprise to us that the ultimate reason for Paul's refusal to keep silent, the basis of his boldness, was his desire to draw ever greater and more vivid attention to God.

Trace it back, step by step. Thanksgiving glorifies God as the giver of all good things. But people cannot give thanks if they do not experience saving grace. And people cannot experience saving grace unless someone, for their sake (v. 15), boldly proclaims the truth of the gospel. My faith is fixed in this truth, Paul says, and thus I speak (v. 13).

Perhaps Paul, in his own way, may have on more than one occasion uttered words similar to Luther's: "My conscience is bound to the Word of God: I cannot and I will not recant anything, since it is unsafe and dangerous to do anything against the conscience. Here I stand. I cannot do otherwise. God help me. Amen!"

Do you believe? Then speak.

Gazing Intently at What You Can't See

2 Corinthians 4:16–18

So we do not lose heart. Though our outer self is wasting away, our inner self is being renewed day by day. For this light momentary affliction is preparing for us an eternal weight of glory beyond all comparison, as we look not to the things that are seen but to the things that are unseen. For the things that are seen are transient, but the things that are unseen are eternal.

I can't remember who said it or wrote it, but I agree with it: *the power to persevere comes from gazing intently at what you can't see.* Needless to say, that calls for explanation. But the explanation itself requires a context.

The context is Paul's discussion of how we as Christians daily carry about in our bodies the dying of Jesus and do so without succumbing to despair or bitterness. His comments in 2 Corinthians 4:16–18 still have in view the experience he described in verses 8–12, one that entails affliction, perplexity, persecution, and being struck down. What that meant for Paul and his ministry in Corinth might not be the same for you and me, but all of us, in our own unique way, face disappointment and suffering that threaten us with discouragement. So how does one not "lose heart"? Where does one find the power to persevere?

If we're going to profit from Paul's perspective, we first need to understand his terms.

The *outer nature* in verse 16 is not a reference to the *old self* of Romans 6:6 (or Col. 3:9 or Eph. 4:22). The *old self* refers to the moral or ethical dimension of our fallen, unregenerate nature. *Outer nature*, on the other hand, refers to our bodily frame, our physical constitution, our creaturely mortality, the "jar of clay" or "earthen vessel" of 2 Corinthians 4:7. Thus, the "wasting away" of our "outer nature" is most likely a reference once more to the hardships of 2 Corinthians 4:8–9, our carrying about in our bodies the dying of Jesus of verse 10, our being handed over to death of verse 11, and the death that is at work in us of verse 12. The renewal of the "inner nature," therefore, is probably synonymous with what Paul earlier said in 3:18 when he declared that we "are being transformed into the same image from one degree of glory to another. . . ."

What makes this truly remarkable is that these are simultaneous processes! At the same time that Paul was physically weak and materially deprived and oppressed by his enemies, he experienced unparalleled spiritual success (see Heb. 11:32–40)! Lutheran commentator R. C. H. Lenski, put it this way:

> With perfect calmness Paul can watch the destruction of his outer man. What if his enemies hasten the process, yea, bring it to a sudden end by means of a violent death! He loses nothing. The inner man blossoms into new youth, beauty, and strength day by day. This inner renewal is not hindered but only helped by the tribulation that assails the outer man. These "bloody roses" have the sweetest odor. These enemies are only defeating their own end; instead of causing Paul to grow discouraged, his elation is increased.[1]

If you aren't aware of the inner transformation, the outer decimation might well breed bitterness and despair.

Paul explains this in greater detail in verse 17. There he says, in utterly stunning terms, that the persecution he endures and the trials he confronts daily are but "slight momentary affliction"! Paul was no Pollyanna. The suffering in his life was very real, not imaginary, and if viewed only from an earthly or temporal perspective, it would probably be more than any human might endure. But when viewed from the vantage point of eternity, "the suffering took on the opposite hue—it seemed slight and temporary. The eye of faith," notes Murray Harris, "creates a new perspective."[2]

Note carefully the contrasts in view: "momentary" is contrasted with "eternal," "slight" is set over against "weight," and "affliction" is counterbalanced by "glory." Paul uses similar language in Romans 8:18. There he says that "the sufferings of this present time are not worth comparing with the glory that is to be revealed to us."

God is not asking you to treat pain as though it were pleasure or grief as though it were joy, but to bring all earthly adversity into comparison with heavenly glory and thereby be strengthened to endure. Philip Hughes put it thus:

> Christian suffering, however protracted it may be, is only for this present life, which, when compared with the everlasting ages of the glory to which it is leading, is but a passing moment; affliction for Jesus' sake, however crushing it may seem, is in fact light, a weightless trifle, when weighed against the mass of that glory which is the inheritance of all who through grace have been made one with the Son of God.[3]

It's encouraging to know that whatever suffering we might endure now, in this age characterized by pain and injustice, cannot overturn or undermine the purposes of God. "Only those who have no genuine vision of eternity," Paul Barnett said, "think otherwise."[4]

But note well: this inner transformation in the midst of outer decay does not happen automatically. Carefully observe the relation between verse 16 and verse 18. In other words, the renewal Paul describes (v. 16) occurs only while or to the extent that "we look not to the things that are seen but to the things that are unseen. For the things that are seen are transient, but the things that are unseen are eternal" (v. 18).

As we fix the gaze of our hearts on the glorious hope of the age to come, God progressively renews our inner being, notwithstanding the simultaneous decay of our outer being. Also note that this is no fleeting or casual glance or occasional thought concerning the "glory" of the age to come. The apostle has in mind a fixity of gaze, an attentive and studious concentration on the inestimable blessings of heaven.

When Paul refers to "the things that are seen," he does not mean material or physical things, as if to suggest that "matter" is evil or unprofitable. God created "matter"! All things were pronounced "good" (Genesis 1). After all, we will live forever on a new "earth" that will be quite tangible and physical. Rather, the contrast between "the things that are seen" and "the things that are unseen" has in view the distinction between the present age and all that is temporal and subject to sin and decay, as over against the unchanging righteousness and incorruptible reality of the age to come.

So don't use this passage to justify a careless, indifferent, or neglectful disregard for the daily responsibilities of life in the present day. Paul is simply warning us against a carnal fixation on what this world system can provide and calling us to set our hope and confidence on the eternal values of God's kingdom.

Here, then, is the power to persevere: by setting your mind and fixing your gaze and focusing your heart on the unseen yet eternal realities of what God has secured for you in Christ. If I may be allowed to turn the age-old and misguided adage on its head, you will never be of much earthly good unless you are utterly heavenly minded.

26

What Happens
When a Christian Dies? (1)

2 Corinthians 5:1–5

For we know that if the tent that is our earthly home is destroyed, we have a building from God, a house not made with hands, eternal in the heavens. For in this tent we groan, longing to put on our heavenly dwelling, if indeed by putting it on we may not be found naked. For while we are still in this tent, we groan, being burdened—not that we would be unclothed, but that we would be further clothed, so that what is mortal may be swallowed up by life. He who has prepared us for this very thing is God, who has given us the Spirit as a guarantee.

I'm dying. I don't say that because I've just returned from the doctor with a fatal diagnosis of cancer or heart disease, but I am dying. So, too, are you. With each passing moment, no matter how vigorously we exercise and how nutritiously we eat, we are deteriorating physically. As Paul said in 2 Corinthians 4:16, "our outer self is wasting away." Nevertheless, and for this we praise God, "our inner self is being renewed day by day" (v. 16).

But death is approaching, for some faster than others. I recently attended the funeral service of a dear friend who lived only fifty years. She left behind a loving and faithful husband and a teenaged son. Much was said at the service about where she is now and what she is experiencing, all to encourage those present who must now face life in her absence.

So where is my friend? What is it, precisely, that she now sees and feels and experiences, or is she, as some would argue, "asleep," unconscious, lifeless in the grave until the second coming of Christ? The most explicit answer to this question, in all of Scripture, is found in 2 Corinthians 5:1–10. We will devote several meditations to a serious consideration of this most important issue: What happens when a Christian dies?

I've witnessed a lot of death in my family in recent years: my father-in-law, a cousin, one uncle, and three aunts have passed away. All were Christians. Like you, I want rock-solid, revelatory assurance, not merely speculation, about where they are. Twice in this paragraph Paul speaks with unshakable confidence, declaring that "we know" (vv. 1, 6) what has happened to them and where they are.

It's important that we read 2 Corinthians 5:1 in the light of what has preceded in 4:7–18. Paul writes, "For we know that if the tent that is our earthly home is destroyed, we have a building from God, a house not made with hands, eternal in the heavens" (5:1). The "tent" or "earthly home," that is, the physical body, is one example of the many "transient" things "that are seen" (4:18), just as "the building from God" is one example of the "eternal" things "that are unseen" (4:18). Similarly, the destruction of the earthly body is simply the ultimate outcome of what Paul described as his repeated encounters with death or his carrying about in himself the dying of Jesus (4:8–12).

What is this "building from God" that is ours following physical death? Among the many possible answers, four are most frequently suggested.

Some argue it is a reference to heaven itself, or an abode in heaven (see John 14:2), perhaps even the New Jerusalem. Others say it refers to the body of Christ, that is, the church. Still others say it may refer to an intermediate body, that is, a bodily form of some sort suitable to the intermediate state but different from and only preparatory to the final, glorified, resurrected body (see Matt. 17:3; Rev. 6:9–11). The fourth option is to see here a reference to the glorified, resurrection body, that final and consummate embodiment in which we will live for eternity.

There are two fundamental reasons for embracing the fourth option and understanding Paul as referring to the final resurrection body (see Phil. 3:21). First, the "house" in verse 1b stands in a parallel relationship with "home" in verse 1a. Since the latter refers to our earthly, unglorified body, it seems reasonable to conclude that the former refers to our heavenly, glorified body. Second, the description in verse 1b ("not made with hands," "eternal," and "in the heavens") is more suitable to the glorified body (see esp. 1 Cor. 15:35–49). Paul's point would be that our heavenly embodiment is indestructible, not susceptible to decay or corruption or dissolution.

The major objection to this view is Paul's use of the present tense: "we *have* a building from God" (not "we *shall* have"). This seems to imply that immediately upon death the believer receives his or her glorified body.

But this would conflict with 1 Corinthians 15 and 1 Thessalonians 4–5, which indicate that glorification occurs at the second advent of Christ. Furthermore, frequently in Scripture an author is so certain and assured of a future reality or possession that he appropriately speaks of it in the present tense, that is, as if it were already ours in experience. Thus Paul's present tense "we have" most likely points to the *fact* of having as well as the *permanency* of having, but not the *immediacy* of having. It is the language of hope.

Some have argued that perhaps Paul uses the present tense because the passing of time between physical death and the final resurrection is not sensed or consciously experienced by the saints in heaven, and thus the reception of one's resurrection body *appears* to follow immediately upon death.

But against this is the clear teaching of Scripture that those who have died consciously experience the intermediate state (as we will soon see in 2 Cor. 5:6–8; cf. Phil. 1:21–24; Rev. 6:9–11). It is clear that the deceased believer has departed to be "with Christ" (Phil. 1:23) and is therefore "with" Christ when he comes (1 Thess. 4:14).

It would seem, then, that some kind of conscious existence obtains between a person's death and the general resurrection (this is why we refer to this time as the *intermediate state*).

Even though Paul appears to envision the possibility (probability?) of his own physical death, he still has hope that he will remain alive until Christ returns.

In 2 Corinthians 5:2–5 Paul speaks of his desire to be alive when Christ returns, for then he would not have to die physically and experience the separation of body and spirit, a condition he refers to as being "naked" (v. 3) or "unclothed" (v. 4). Paul's perspective on life and death may therefore be put in this way:

It is *good* to remain alive on this earth to serve Christ (see Phil. 1:21–26).

On the other hand, it is *better* to die physically and enter into the presence of Christ (see 2 Cor. 5:6–8; Phil. 1:21b, 23).

However, it is by far and away *best* to be alive when Christ returns, for then we avoid death altogether and are immediately joined with the Lord in our resurrected and glorified bodies.

In verse 2 (which is repeated and expanded somewhat in v. 4) Paul mixes his metaphors by speaking of putting on or being "clothed" with a "building." But it is more than simply putting on a garment: it is putting on a garment *over* another. The heavenly body, like an outer vesture or overcoat, is being put on over the earthly body with which the apostle is, as it were, presently clad. In this way the heavenly, glorified body not only covers but also absorbs and *transforms* the earthly one (see Phil. 3:20–21; 1 Cor. 15:53).

If Paul remains alive until Christ returns, he will be found by the Lord clothed with a body (the present, earthly one), and not in a disembodied state (v. 3). To be without a body is to be "naked." Clearly, Paul envisaged a state of disembodiment between physical death and the general resurrection (see "unclothed" in v. 4).

But what assurances do we have from God that he will in fact supply us with a glorified and eternal body that is no longer subject to the deterioration and disease we now experience? The simple answer is: the Holy Spirit! Paul's statement in verse 5 is a reminder "that 'the earnest of the Spirit' is not a mere static deposit, but the active vivifying operation of the Holy Spirit within the believer, assuring him that the same principle of power which effected the resurrection of Christ Jesus from the dead is also present and at work within him, preparing his mortal body for the consummation of his redemption in the glorification of his body."[1]

For the Christian, death is not to be feared. For we know that whatever illness or debilitation we experience now, whatever degree of suffering or hardship we must face, there is promised to us by the Spirit a glorified, Christlike, transformed, and utterly eternal abode, a body in which there is no disease, no pain, no deprivation, and no decay.

"The best-case scenario," Paul seems to say, "is to be alive when Christ returns. That way I could transition instantaneously from this 'garment' (my current physical body) into that glorified 'vesture' (that is and will forever be my resurrected body). I don't want to get 'undressed' but to put the garment of eternity over the garment of time in such a way that the former redeems and transforms the latter. But in all things I yield to the timing and purpose of God, and rejoice in the assurance, the rock-solid guarantee from the Holy Spirit, that physical death is not the end but the beginning."

"Therefore encourage one another with these words" (1 Thess. 4:18).

27

What Happens
When a Christian Dies? (2)

2 Corinthians 5:6–8

So we are always of good courage. We know that while we are at home in the body we are away from the Lord, for we walk by faith, not by sight. Yes, we are of good courage, and we would rather be away from the body and at home with the Lord.

L et us consider this settled," John Calvin said, "that no one has made progress in the school of Christ who does not joyfully await the day of death and final resurrection."[1] All non-Christians and, sadly, some professing believers, would regard that as a statement of unparalleled lunacy. For them, the "day of death" is something to dread, the prospect of which evokes fear and the avoidance of which justifies any sacrifice, even that of truth and virtue.

So how can it be not only a sign of sanity but of spiritual maturity to "joyfully" await and eagerly long for the "day of death"? It couldn't, were it not for such remarkable passages as 2 Corinthians 5:6–8.

The point of the passage is simple enough: far from being an experience of dreary darkness and unremitting despair, death for the Christian means immediate entrance into the glorious light of the presence of Jesus Christ.

I vividly remember the first time I watched a person die. I had been called, on countless occasions, to the home or hospital room of someone who earlier had passed away, but not until I actually watched a man breathe his last breath did this passage in 2 Corinthians strike me with full force.

Not so much as a nanosecond beyond his final breath, he was gazing directly, joyfully, painlessly, and eternally into the eyes of his Savior, the Lord Jesus Christ. Fully conscious and wholly free, he fell rapturously into the arms of the one who, from then and forevermore, would never let him go.

This is the rock-solid assurance, the blood-bought promise, signed, sealed, and delivered by the unshakable guarantee of the Holy Spirit (2 Cor. 5:5), of every born-again believer in Jesus Christ. A close look at these three verses is clearly warranted.

We begin with the observation that while verses 6 and 8 should be read together, verse 7 is a parenthetical explanation of the end of verse 6 (more on this below). Paul couldn't have said it with greater clarity: to be *in the body* (i.e., physically alive) is to be *absent from the Lord* and to be *out of the body* (i.e., physically dead) is to be *present with the Lord.*

Paul's point is that as one must be either in or out of his body (for there is no third alternative), so he must be either absent from or present with the Lord (for, again, there is no third alternative). To the question, "when a Christian dies does he or she *immediately* enter Christ's presence?" the answer must be "yes." Three things support this conclusion.

First, in verse 6, residence in a physical body is contemporaneous with absence from the direct presence of Christ, implying that when the former ceases so also does the latter. Observe the temporal indicators: "*while* we are at home in the body *we are* away from the Lord." And what verse 6 may only imply, verse 8 explicitly asserts: "we would rather be *away from the body* and *at home with the Lord.*"

Second, according to verse 7, walking by faith and walking by sight are the only two possible ways of relating to Christ. When the former ends, the latter begins. We now walk by faith, in the sense that we can't see him. But when we die, faith gives way to sight, not that we cease to believe in him but in the sense that we add to faith the experience of literal, visible communion. In other words, "the separation . . . is relative not absolute: though absent from sight, the Lord is present to faith, yet it is not until he is present also to sight that Christian existence will reach its true goal of consummated fellowship with him."[2]

Don't be misled by this verse. Paul is not suggesting that we are now bereft of communion with Christ or that it is merely illusory. It is simply incomplete or imperfect. Being physically alive is not an obstacle to true spirituality. We can still know Christ and enjoy him, as Peter makes clear in chapter 1 of his first epistle: "Though you have not seen him, you love him. Though you do not now see him, you believe in him and rejoice with joy that is inexpressible and filled with glory" (1 Pet. 1:8).

The difference between the "dead in Christ" (believers who have died and gone to be with the Lord) and living Christians is not one of status, as if to say the former are "truly saved" or "more in Christ" than the latter. Rather, it is, first, a difference of disembodiment versus embodiment. Second, it is a difference in "the *quality* of their fellowship with Christ and the *degree* of their proximity to Christ."[3]

Therefore, 2 Corinthians 5:7 is designed to soften the blow of the end of verse 6, or to explain in what sense being "in" the body entails "absence" from Christ. Our absence from Christ is only *spatial, not spiritual* (see Matt. 28:19–20; Col. 1:27; John 17:23, 26). While in the body we do not literally *see* Christ, but rather we walk by faith in the physically absent and unseen Lord. Death brings us into spatial proximity and visible contact with Christ. Thus death, rather than severing our spiritual relationship with Christ, heightens and enhances it! Death brings us into the immediate vision of our Savior and the increased intimacy of fellowship that it entails.

Third, that the believer's physical death issues immediately in conscious presence with the Lord is Paul's teaching in Philippians

137

1:20–24. There Paul describes the tension he feels between wanting, on the one hand, "to depart [i.e., die physically] and be with Christ," and, on the other, to remain "in the flesh" [i.e., physically alive] so that he might engage in "fruitful labor" on behalf of the churches he has established. Adolphe Monod has beautifully captured the perspective of Paul, one that is often missing in the church today:

> Before that, the apostle wonders which is better for him, to live or to die. This question has often come before us, and perhaps we have answered like the apostle. But it is to be feared that we meant it in quite a different way. If we preferred death, then it meant, "I do not know which I should dread the most, the afflictions of life from which death would deliver me, or the terrors of death from which life preserves me." We mean that life and death appear to us as two evils, and we do not know which of them is the lesser evil. As for the apostle, they both appear to him as two immense blessings and he does not know which is the better of them![4]

Several important theological implications should be noted.

First, what becomes of the Roman Catholic doctrine of purgatory, according to which the Christian at death must endure additional purification from sin before entering the bliss of Christ's presence? Clearly it is eliminated.[5]

Second, what does this mean for the doctrine of soul sleep, or *psychopannychia*, which asserts that Christians at death enter a state of complete unconsciousness, to be "awakened" at Christ's return? It, too, is eliminated. What, then, does the New Testament mean when it refers to death as "sleep" (see Matt. 27:52; Luke 8:52; John 11:11–13; Acts 7:60; 1 Cor. 7:39; 11:30; 15:6, 18; 1 Thess. 4:13)?

Several things come to mind. For example, sleep implies rest from earthly toil, the cessation of activity in *this* realm. Thus one is asleep to *this* world, but alive and very much "awake" in the next. The imagery of sleep is also used to describe death because the *body* does sleep, in a manner of speaking. In other words, the body is at rest, without activity or life. But nowhere does the Bible say that the "soul" or "spirit" sleeps or is unconscious. Finally, sleep is used to illustrate that the pain of death as a penalty for sin is gone for the Christian. Death for the believer, rather than something to be feared, is like dozing off for a nap (see Luke 16:19–31; Matt. 17:1–8; Mark 12:26–27; Rev. 6:9–11).

John Calvin was right: we cannot claim to have progressed very far in Christ if we do not look forward with great joy and expectation to the day of death, for then we will see in unmediated vision and enjoy with unparalleled bliss the Jesus in whom, until then, we could but believe.

Finally, a word is in order for those who have suffered the loss of a believing spouse, child, friend, or family member.

Countless are the times, following a funeral, that I have been asked: "Where are they now? What are they experiencing?" And it has been my great joy to say, with complete and unshaken confidence: "They are with Jesus, in his presence, beholding his beauty, enthralled by his splendor, breathless with unbroken joy, adding their voice to that of the four living creatures and the twenty-four elders and the myriads of angels and the multitude of the redeemed, singing 'Holy, holy, holy, is the Lord God Almighty, who was and is and is to come!'" (Rev. 4:8).

28

What Happens
When a Christian Dies? (3)

2 Corinthians 5:9–10

So whether we are at home or away, we make it our aim to please
him. For we must all appear before the judgment seat of Christ,
so that each one may receive what is due for what he has done in
the body, whether good or evil.

To this point in our study of what happens when a Christian
dies, most everyone is pleased with what Paul has written. So
why spoil everything by talking about judgment? I can antici-
pate what some people will say: "I was thrilled when you described
the reality of the intermediate state and the assurance of bodily
resurrection. I was ecstatic upon hearing that to be absent from the
body is to be present with the Lord. But judgment? Couldn't you
have conveniently skipped over that one?"

Well, no, I couldn't. Paul didn't, so neither can we.

Let's be clear about one thing from the start, something that I
believe may go a long way in putting to rest someone's fears about
judgment. In one of the most encouraging and liberating texts in the
New Testament, Paul wrote: "There is therefore now *no condemna-*

1

tion for those who are in Christ Jesus" (Rom. 8:1). In other words, whatever else Paul may have in mind in 2 Corinthians 5, if you are "in Christ Jesus" by faith you need never, ever fear condemnation. That being said and settled, what ought we to expect, following death, at the judgment seat of Christ?

The best way to answer this question is with a series of ten observations Paul's statement evokes.

First, *who* is to be judged? Whereas it is possible that all mankind are included here, the broader context in 2 Corinthians 4–5 suggests that believers only are in view. Murray Harris has also pointed out that wherever Paul speaks of the recompense, according to works, of all people (such as in Rom. 2:6), "there is found a description of two mutually exclusive categories of people (Rom. 2:7–10), not a delineation of two types of action [such as "whether good or evil" here in v. 10] which may be predicated of all people."[1]

Second, what is the *nature* or *purpose* of the judgment? In view of Romans 8:1, as well as John 3:18; 5:24; Romans 5:8–9; and 1 Thessalonians 1:10 (to mention just a few), eternal destiny is not at issue; eternal reward is. This judgment is not designed to determine entrance into the kingdom of God but reward or status or authority within it. More on this below.

Third, *when* does this judgment occur? At the moment of physical death? During the intermediate state? At the second coming of Christ? Paul doesn't seem concerned to specify when. The most that we can be sure of is that it happens after death (see Heb. 9:27). Having said that, I'm inclined to think it happens at the second coming of Christ (see Matt. 16:27; Rev. 22:12), at the close of human history, most likely in conjunction with that larger assize that will include all unbelievers, known to students of the Bible as the Great White Throne judgment (see Rev. 20:11–15).

Fourth, we should take note of the *inevitability* of judgment for everyone ("we *must all* appear"). This is not a day that can be set aside as irrelevant or unnecessary. It is essential for God to bring to consummation his redemptive purpose and to fully honor the glory of his name among his people.

No one is exempt. Paul himself anticipated standing at this judgment, for it served (at least in part) as the motivation for his grace-energized efforts to "please" the Lord (v. 9).

Fifth, Paul emphasizes its *individuality* ("each one"). As important as it is to stress the corporate and communal nature of our life as the body of Christ, each person will be judged individually (no doubt, at least in part, concerning how faithful each person was to his or her corporate responsibilities!). Paul said it in similar terms in Romans 14:12: "So then *each of us* will give an account of *himself* to God."

Sixth, we should observe the *mode* or *manner* of this judgment ("we must all *appear*"). We do not merely "show up" at the judgment seat of Christ but are *laid bare* before him. As Paul said in 1 Corinthians 4:5, the Lord "will bring to light the things now hidden in darkness and will disclose the purposes of the heart. . . ." Harris is right that "not merely an appearance or self-revelation, but, more significantly, a divine scrutiny and disclosure, is the necessary prelude to the receiving of appropriate recompense."[2]

Is it not sobering to think that every random thought, every righteous impulse, every secret prayer, hidden deed, long-forgotten sin, or act of compassion will be brought into the open for us to acknowledge and for the Lord to judge? But don't forget: "There is therefore now *no condemnation* for those who are in Christ Jesus" (Rom. 8:1)!

Seventh, this judgment has an *identity* all its own (it is the "*judgment seat* of Christ"). Many Christians are familiar with the term used here: *bema*. The use of this word in verse 10 "would have been particularly evocative for Paul and the Corinthians since it was before Gallio's tribunal in Corinth that Paul had stood some four years previously (in AD 52) when the proconsul dismissed the charge that Paul had contravened Roman law (Acts 18:12–17). Archaeologists have identified this Corinthian *bema* which stands on the south side of the *agora*."[3]

Eighth, the *judge* himself is clearly identified (it is the "judgment seat of *Christ*"). This is consistent with what we read in John 5:22 where Jesus said that "the Father judges no one, but has given all judgment to the Son."

Ninth, of critical importance is the *standard* of judgment ("what he has done in the body, whether good or evil"). Reference to the "body" indicates that the judgment concerns what we do in this life, not what may or may not be done during the time of the intermediate state itself.

According to the ESV, we receive "what is due." In other words, and somewhat more literally, we will be judged "in accordance with" or perhaps even "in proportion to" deeds done. The deeds are themselves characterized as either "good" (those which "please" Christ) or "bad" (those which do not please him).

Tenth, the *result* of the judgment is not explicitly stated but is certainly implied. All will "receive" whatever their deeds deserve. There is a reward or recompense involved. Paul is slightly more specific in 1 Corinthians 3:14–15: "If the work that anyone has built on the foundation survives, he will receive a reward. If anyone's work is burned up, he will suffer loss, though he himself will be saved, but only as through fire." The "reward" is not defined, and the likelihood is that the "loss" suffered is the "reward" that he or she would otherwise have received had they obeyed.

Can anything more definitive be said about the nature of this recompense? Jesus mentions a "great" reward in heaven, but doesn't elaborate (Matt. 5:11–12). In the parable of the talents (Matt. 25; cf. Luke 19:12–27) he alludes to "authority" or dominion of some sort (but over whom or what?). Paul says that "whatever good anyone does, this he will receive back from the Lord . . . (Eph. 6:8).

According to 1 Corinthians 4:5, following the judgment "each one will receive his commendation from God." Both Romans 8:17–18 and 2 Corinthians 4:17 refer to a glory that is reserved for the saints in heaven. And of course we should consider the many promises in the seven letters to the churches in Revelation 2–3, although it is difficult to know if they are bestowed now, during the intermediate state, or only subsequent to the second coming, and if they are granted in differing degrees depending on service and obedience or are equally distributed among God's children (see Rev. 2:7, 10, 17, 23; 3:5, 12, 21; cf. Matt. 18:4; 19:29; Luke 14:11; James 1:12).

Perhaps the differing nature and degree of reward will be manifest in the depths of knowledge and enjoyment of God that each person experiences. People often balk at this notion, but they shouldn't. Here is how I explained it in my book, *One Thing*.

> Hardly anything will bring you more joy [in heaven] than to see other saints with greater rewards than you, experiencing greater glory than you, given greater authority than you! There will be no jealousy or pride to fuel your unhealthy competitiveness. There will be no greed to energize your race to get more than everyone else. *You will then delight only in delighting in the delight of others. Their achievement will be your greatest joy. Their success will be your highest happiness.* You will truly rejoice with those who rejoice. Envy comes from lack. But in heaven there is no lack. Whatever you need, you get. Whatever desires may arise, they are satisfied.
>
> The fact that some are more holy and more happy than others will not diminish the joy of the latter. There will be perfect humility and perfect resignation to God's will in heaven, hence no resentment or bitterness. Also, those higher in holiness will, precisely because they are holy, be more humble. The essence of holiness is humility! The very vice that might incline them to look condescendingly on those lower than themselves is nowhere present. It is precisely because they are more holy that they are so very humble and thus incapable of arrogance and elitism.
>
> They will not strut or boast or use their higher degrees of glory to humiliate or harm those lower. Those who know more of God will, because of that knowledge, think more lowly and humbly of themselves. They will be more aware of the grace that accounts for their holiness than those who know and experience less of God, hence, they will be more ready to serve and to yield and to go low and to defer.
>
> Some people in heaven will be happier than others. But this is no reason for sadness or anger. In fact, *it will serve only to make you happier to see that others are more happy than you! Your happiness will increase when you see that the happiness of others has exceeded your own.* Why? Because love dominates in heaven and love is rejoicing in the increase of the happiness of others. To love someone is to desire their greatest joy. As their joy increases, so too does yours in them. If their joy did not increase, neither would yours. We struggle with this because now on earth our thoughts and desires and motives are corrupted by sinful self-seeking, competitiveness, envy, jealousy, and resentment.[4]

Two closing comments are in order. First, our deeds do not determine our salvation, but demonstrate it. They are not the root of our standing with God but the fruit of it, a standing already attained by faith alone in Christ alone. The visible evidence of an invisible faith are the "good" deeds that will be made known at the judgment seat of Christ.

Second, don't be afraid that, with the exposure and evaluation of your deeds, regret and remorse will spoil the bliss of heaven. If there be tears of grief for opportunities squandered, or tears of shame for sins committed, he will wipe them away (Rev. 21:4). The ineffable joy of forgiving grace will swallow up all sorrow, and the beauty of Christ will blind you to anything other than the splendor of who he is and what he has, by grace, accomplished on your behalf.

29

You, Others, and the Judgment Seat of Christ

2 Corinthians 5:11–12

Therefore, knowing the fear of the Lord, we persuade others. But what we are is known to God, and I hope it is known also to your conscience. We are not commending ourselves to you again but giving you cause to boast about us, so that you may be able to answer those who boast about outward appearance and not about what is in the heart.

The inescapable reality of the judgment seat of Christ (2 Cor. 5:10) is a sobering thing. It takes hold of the heart and forces us to think about what we cherish and how we speak and what we do and the many and varied ways that we use our time and money and energy and gifts.

But what effect, if any, does it have on your responsibility toward others? It's easy to become self-absorbed when thinking about judgment and recompense for deeds done in this life. But what about others? What effect does it have on your heart to contemplate your family and friends and fellow church members standing before the *bema* of Christ?

You are undoubtedly aware, as I am, of people who profess to know Christ who are languishing in spiritual mediocrity. You may be in close fellowship with several who appear unconcerned about the truths that Paul has articulated here in 2 Corinthians 5. While Paul spoke of his aim "to please" the Lord (v. 9), knowing that his life would soon come under the scrutiny of divine judgment, they seem only to shrug indifferently.

How do you respond to that? Do you casually dismiss their apathy, reminding yourself that you've got enough to deal with in your own life without getting involved in the struggles of someone else?

Paul's attitude was altogether of a different order and dictated a radically other-oriented agenda for life and ministry.

Let's first be clear about what Paul has in mind when he speaks of "the fear of the Lord" (v. 11).

This isn't the fear that unbelievers should feel as they contemplate the eternal judgment that awaits them, but rather the fear of the *Christian* at the prospect of standing before the Lord to have his or her deeds scrutinized and recompensed. It is the fear of not pleasing the Lord, to which Paul earlier referred in verse 9. It is the fear of one's works being assessed as "evil" (v. 10) and thus suffering the loss of that reward that would otherwise have come with obedience to the will and ways of God.

It is because Paul is gripped with this fear that he persuades men. But whom does Paul labor to persuade, and of what?

Often people simply assume he is referring to gospel ministry and his efforts to persuade the lost that Jesus is Lord (see Acts 18:4; 19:8; 28:23). Or, given Paul's purpose in 2 Corinthians, he may have in mind his persuasion of the Corinthian church of his integrity as a man and his authenticity as an apostle (see 2 Cor. 3:1–6; 4:1–6).

But the word "therefore" with which verse 11 opens links Paul's persuasive efforts to what he has just articulated in verses 1–10, especially verses 9–10. In other words, it is the Corinthians themselves (and of course all people by reasonable extension) whom Paul seeks to persuade to live in such a way that Christ is pleased and they are properly rewarded at the judgment seat. This interpretation is also confirmed by what Paul says in verse 15. There he affirms that Christ "died for all, that those who live might *no longer live for themselves but for him* who for their sake died and was raised."

Consider this extended paraphrase of Paul's argument:

> There is no escaping the judgment seat of Christ. All of us who profess to know him as Savior will one day give an account for every deed and every word. That is why we must strive, in his grace, to please him in everything we do. This is a sobering thought, but not because we fear that he will reject us eternally (let's not forget Rom. 8:1!). Nevertheless, we don't want to squander opportunities for ministry or waste our lives in fruitless activities. The idea of standing before the Lord and being recompensed for the good and evil we have done is enough to instill within me a deep and abiding trembling and fearful awe of having failed to please him. Knowing this impels me to persuade you and others to live in holiness and obedience and wholehearted commitment to please him in all things. Indeed, given the fact that he has died for us, ought we not to live for him rather than for ourselves (v. 15)?

Therefore, the "fear" of the Lord is not the fear of *condemnation* but of less than notable *commendation* when our deeds are assessed on the day of judgment.

This doesn't mean that Paul's primary goal is to justify himself before God (v. 11b). His life and ministry are already seen and known by the omniscient God before whom all things are laid bare. Nor is he justifying himself in the eyes of the Corinthians. After all, the authenticity of who he is has already been made known to their consciences (vv. 11b–12a; cf. 3:1–3).

Rather, Paul's aim is to provide the Corinthians with whatever evidence they need to refute those in the church who are bent on questioning Paul's integrity and thereby undermining his apostolic claims (v. 12). As Scott Hafemann has explained,

> Paul's opponents took pride in their professional rhetorical prowess, their letters of recommendation from other churches, the payment they received for their ministry, their ethnic and spiritual pedigree, and their ecstatic spiritual experiences. These are the external things that "are seen" (5:12); that is, they are on the surface (cf. 10:7). As in 3:2 and 4:2, here too Paul maintains that his opponents' focus on

such externals mask the true nature of their motives, whereas his own actions reveal the genuine nature of his "heart."[1]

Let me conclude with an exhortation. When you've finished meditating on this passage and the divine scrutiny of your own life at the judgment seat of Christ, turn your thoughts to others. I have in mind those individuals you've conveniently ignored who have professed Christ as Savior but seem spiritually indifferent. Perhaps they've slacked off on church attendance or haven't shown up for small group in more than a month. It may be that they've yielded to the pressure of coworkers and have begun to turn their Christian liberty into license. Or perhaps they're even contemplating an extramarital affair.

Go to them, appeal to them, encourage and "persuade" them that the reality of the judgment seat of Christ cannot be denied. Offer yourself to them as someone who will labor side by side as an accountability partner. Commit yourself to pray for them daily. Meet with them often. Remind them, lovingly and firmly, that Christ died for sinners so that "those who live might no longer live for themselves but *for him* who for their sake died and was raised" (v. 15).

If indeed we know "the fear of the Lord," how can we possibly do otherwise? James put it best in saying, "My brothers, if anyone among you wanders from the truth and someone brings him back, let him know that whoever brings back a sinner from his wandering will save his soul from death and will cover a multitude of sins" (James 5:19–20).

30

"Out of His Mind" for God

2 Corinthians 5:13

For if we are beside ourselves, it is for God; if we are in our right mind, it is for you.

There's hardly anything more painful and disheartening than being misunderstood. I can't begin to imagine what Jesus must have felt each time the religious leaders twisted his words into something he never intended or misinterpreted his motives or impugned his character, attributing to him ideas or aims foreign to his heart.

The apostle Paul was another who often experienced this kind of misunderstanding. His actions often ran counter to the cultural norms of his day, not least of which was his refusal to accept remuneration from any church in which he was at that time ministering (although he had every right to be supported by them, as he makes clear in 1 Cor. 9:3–18).

Here in 2 Corinthians 5, Paul refers explicitly to being the object of this sort of unwarranted misinterpretation. He has acknowledged that he does not follow the ways of the false teachers in Corinth who parade their "outward appearance" as grounds for boasting (v. 12; would that our Christian leaders and TV personalities might hear

150

150

and heed this word!). This inevitably exposed Paul to accusations that he was out of his mind, although in the final analysis he couldn't have cared less what they thought of him. That is why here, in the flow of his argument, he declares, "For if we are beside ourselves, it is for God; if we are in our right mind, it is for you" (2 Cor. 5:13).

Paul's point is that self-interest simply doesn't factor into his decisions or behavior. If he is judged irrational or insane, that is between him and God. If he is considered rational and astute, it is for the welfare of others. But before I go any further, a comment is in order about Paul's choice of terms in this text.

The word translated "beside ourselves" is *exestemen*. Paul uses it nowhere else, but we find it in Mark 3:21 where it refers to Jesus! There we read, "And when his family heard it, they went out to seize him, for they were saying, 'He is *out of his mind*.'" The New Testament also uses this word as an expression of amazement (see Matt. 12:23; Mark 2:12; Luke 8:56; Acts 2:7, 12; 8:13; 9:21; 10:45; 12:16).

Paul's statement has thus been interpreted in a number of ways. Some argue that his critics were insisting that he was a victim of religious mania—that he had lost his senses, a criticism that may have been due to certain doctrines he proposed. You may recall at his trial that Festus declared "with a loud voice, 'Paul, you are out of your mind; your great learning is driving you out of your mind'" (Acts 26:24). Of course, Paul's response was to say, "I am not out of my mind, most excellent Festus, but I am speaking true and rational words" (Acts 26:25).

This charge may also have been provoked by the apostle's "indefatigable zeal and tireless work (cf. 6:4–5; 11:23–28),"[1] his unbridled passion for Jesus, and the extreme physical and emotional abuse to which he willingly exposed himself for the sake of the gospel (see 2 Cor. 4:7–18; 6:4–10). Perhaps his opponents in Corinth thought Paul too eccentric for their own tastes, preferring instead someone who would diligently uphold the norms of social propriety. Paul, quite simply, lacked those social graces they regarded as essential for a true apostle.

Another option is that Paul is referring to exaggerated behavior in his past that he now repudiates. His point would be that however extreme or bizarre his actions may have been, God knows they were well-meant and sincere.

A final option is that Paul has in view here his own personal experience of what some have called "religious ecstasy" or "spiritual elation." Included would be his consistent and unapologetic practice of praying in tongues, for which he gives God profound thanks (1 Cor. 14:18; although be it noted that tongues is nowhere described as "ecstatic" in the New Testament), as well as his many dreams, visions, and trances (see Acts 16:6–10; 18:9–22; 22:17). Some would also point to his having been caught up into the third heaven, as he will later describe in 2 Corinthians 12.

In the final analysis, it matters little which view is embraced. What is important is that in the immediately preceding verse (2 Cor. 5:12), Paul distanced himself from those who were obsessed with "outward appearance," which is to say, they took pride in their credentials and wanted to be perceived as "having it all together."

Paul, on the other hand, put no stock in such claims. For him, it was solely a matter of "the heart" (v. 12), of inward integrity and sincerity in conduct. That his behavior may well have appeared bizarre, extreme, and outlandish by the standards of most was of no concern to him. If his conduct evoked charges of being crazy, he was willing to live with it, so long as God was honored.

His point is that all he does is either for the glory of God or for the spiritual welfare of other believers. He simply does not take himself into consideration. No matter what his state of mind may be, self promotion does not factor into his aims or activities. "If he had visionary experiences—on which his opponents prided themselves—they were moments of intimacy between God and himself, and not to be paraded as flamboyant claims."[2] If, on the other hand, he appears right-minded and rational, that is for the sake of the Corinthians themselves and their spiritual edification. But nothing is done with himself in view, even though he may be the victim of unjustified caricature.

Let's return now to what's most important for us to learn from the apostle in this passage. If God is being honored and exalted, what difference does it make what others may think? Our value as individuals is not suspended on the approval of religious elites. Paul had two primary concerns, neither of which was his own reputation. He cared only that God be honored in his life and that other Christians be edified by his ministry.

So, how do you respond to unwarranted criticism? What reaction is evoked when your motives are misinterpreted? Is either your life or ministry dependent on the approval of men, or do you seek God's favor alone? Whether we are maligned as madmen or eulogized for our eloquence, our aim should be the glory of God and the good of his people. Nothing else matters.

31

The Controlling Power of the Cross

2 Corinthians 5:14–15

For the love of Christ controls us, because we have concluded this: that one has died for all, therefore all have died; and he died for all, that those who live might no longer live for themselves but for him who for their sake died and was raised.

What gets you going in the morning? Aside from an alarm clock and the prospect of being fired from your job should you choose to remain in bed, what energizes you to face each day? How do you account for your decision to press on in life when there seem to be so many reasons to quit?

Do you find yourself coerced by an external force, perhaps a threat, a promise, or the hope of winning the lottery (that's not an endorsement to purchase a ticket)? Is your life defined by the expectations of others or the fear of what may befall you should you choose to renege on your obligations?

The apostle Paul was a driven man, a man with seemingly endless energy, a man who gave every appearance to those who knew him of being impelled by an unseen power. How else do we explain his life, especially as it is portrayed in the book of 2 Corinthians?

I ask this question in view of Paul's own explicit word of testimony concerning the driving force of his daily existence.

Quite clearly *love* is the power that accounts for Paul's remarkable life and willing sacrifice for the church and the glory of God. But *whose* love, and for what? You don't need to understand Greek to see that the phrase in question can be interpreted in one of two ways. Paul is either referring to *his love for Christ* or to *Christ's love for him* (and some would argue that both are in mind!). I'm glad the ESV has chosen not to interpret the phrase for us. In my opinion, that is the task for the student of Scripture.

Although Paul's personal love for the Lord Jesus Christ is passionate and unquestioned, I don't think that is what he has in view. There are at least two reasons why I'm convinced that Paul is referring to the love and affection that Christ has for us.

First, in virtually every other instance where Paul uses this particular construction (a personal genitive [in this case, "of Christ"] after the word "love" [Greek, *agape*]), he refers to the love which that person has or demonstrates or manifests. Thus, when we read about "the love of God" in Romans 5:5 or "the love of Christ" in Romans 8:35 or "the love of the Spirit" in Romans 15:30, it is the Father's love, the Son's love, and the Spirit's love for sinners that Paul has in view.

Second, and perhaps even more important, is the context. Clearly Paul has in mind Christ's death for us (he "died for all") as the preeminent expression of his love. As Paul reflects on the unfathomable sacrifice Christ made for sinners such as himself, he is gripped yet again with "the breadth and length and height and depth" (Eph. 3:18) of divine affection for hell-deserving transgressors. This, then, is the single reality that shapes and sustains and empowers his every breath, every decision, and every sacrifice he made.

The word translated *controls* or *constrains* literally means "hemmed in." It is as if Paul says, "I'm on a road where I can veer neither right nor left. I can't even retreat! I'm pushed forward by the transforming power of knowing that Jesus loved me to such an extent that he would give his life in my place on the cross."

The water that flows in a river has no choice but to follow the direction set by its banks on the right and left. Such is how Paul feels. Thus the idea is far more than that of mere "moral influence" or "persuasion." It's as if Paul says, "If ever I should be tempted to think first of my own welfare, the love of Christ at the cross takes hold of my heart and liberates me *from* myself and *for* the service of others. If ever I should use my suffering as an excuse to slow down or back off or withdraw altogether, Christ's willingness to endure the wrath of God on my behalf lights a flame in my soul that no amount of earthly comfort or promise of man's praise can extinguish!"

Perhaps this doesn't resonate with us as it did with Paul because we don't understand the magnitude of what Christ's death entailed for us. If that is true, let James Denney shed light on the significance of that powerful preposition translated "for":

> Plainly, if *Paul's* conclusion is to be drawn, the "for" must reach deeper than this mere suggestion of our advantage: if we all *died*, in that Christ died *for* us, there must be a sense in which that death of His is *ours*; He must be identified with *us* in it; there, on the cross, while we stand and gaze at Him, He is not simply a person doing us a service; He is a person doing us a service *by filling our place and dying our death*![1]

This, Paul says, accounts for all that I am, all that I do, everything I endure, and everything for which I hope and live. Were it not for the amazing grace and undying love of Christ as manifest in his dying my death, I would degenerate into a self-absorbed solipsist. When I feel self-pity rising up in my heart, I'm reminded of the love of Christ and thereby empowered to slay it. When I find bitterness taking root in my soul, I'm reminded of the love of Christ and thereby impelled to renounce it. And when indifference threatens my commitment, the cross of Christ's love ignites a zeal that sustains me through every trial.

Here is what controls, constrains, and impels me, Paul says: It is that Jesus chose not to hate me (though I was hateful), but to love me (though I was unlovely), and gave himself for me that I might now live for him.

Does the love of God revealed in the cross exert a similar power in your life, or in mine?

When long-held dreams are shattered against the rock of unexpected reality, do you find strength in the knowledge that he died your death so that you might live in the power of his resurrection life?

When others betray or abandon you, are you sustained by the assurance that the cross is the measure of his commitment to you and the pledge, in blood, that he will never leave you or forsake you (see Heb. 13:5)?

Does the reminder that "he who did not spare his own Son but gave him up for" your sake (Rom. 8:32) prove adequate in times of despair and depression and confusion?

I ask you today (as I ask myself): What "constrains" your choices? What "controls" your mind? What animates your affections? What empowers your relationships? I pray that, together with Paul, you can say it is the glorious and incomparable assurance that he "loved me and gave himself for me" (Gal. 2:20).

32

His Love and Our Fear: Can the Two Coexist?

2 Corinthians 5:11, 14

Therefore, knowing the fear of the Lord, we persuade others. But what we are is known to God, and I hope it is known also to your conscience. . . . For the love of Christ controls us, because we have concluded this: that one has died for all, therefore all have died. . . .

Houston, we have a problem." These words made famous by Jim Lovell of Apollo 13 fame may well apply to our efforts to understand something Paul said in 2 Corinthians 5.

Careful students of Scripture will have noted that Paul is describing in chapter 5, among other things, his *motivation* for how he conducted himself among the Corinthians and in the world at large. Yet, he appears to affirm what many would consider mutually incompatible, contradictory ways of relating to God, as well as two reasons or rationales for ministry that seem incapable of existing simultaneously in the same soul. Let's look closely at his words.

In 2 Corinthians 5:11 he spoke of "the fear of the Lord," an obvious reference to *our* fear of *him*. This fear is what moved and stirred his heart to "persuade others" (v. 11). Yet, later in 2 Corinthians 5:14 he speaks of "the love of Christ" (*his* toward *us*) as the controlling or constraining power in his life, a power that shaped and fashioned his every movement and word.

As I said, "Houston, we have a problem!" The problem is the apparent inconsistency of fearing the very One whose love for you is eternal and all-consuming. If Christ loves us in the way Paul describes, a love that led him to offer up himself on our behalf on the cross, what possible role does fear have in our relationship with him?

Did not John the Apostle say "perfect love casts out fear" (1 John 4:18; cf. also Rom. 8:15)? Indeed, he did. It appears, then, that "love" and "fear" are antithetical one to the other. How then can Paul argue that both play a role in motivating him in ministry and governing both why and how he relates to God?

To make sense of this, let's look briefly at this famous passage in 1 John 4:18. In the preceding verse, John wrote: "By this is love perfected with us, so that we may have confidence for the day of judgment, because as he is so also are we in this world" (v. 17).

According to John, God's love has a goal. God does not love us aimlessly. John speaks of God's love being *perfected* or coming to full expression in us. I believe that John is saying much the same that Paul said in Romans 5:5. The Father's love for his children reaches its intended goal when it produces in them a feeling of security so powerful that they lose all fear of judgment. When our sense of being loved by God becomes so *internally intense* that we can only smile at the prospect of judgment day, his passion has fulfilled its purpose.

Someone might think it presumptuous to have lost all fear of judgment. But John clearly says that our confidence is based on the *fact* that the believer is "as he [Jesus] is." What could that possibly mean? In what sense is the Christian "as Jesus is" in the world? John may mean that *we are righteous*, as Jesus is righteous. By faith in him we are justified, declared righteous in the sight of God, and therefore we look forward to judgment day confident that there is now no condemnation for those who are in Christ Jesus (Rom. 8:1). That's possible, but I think the answer lies elsewhere.

Look again at 1 John 4:17. John is saying that our confidence is linked with God's love for us and that in some sense we are as Jesus is. These two pieces of the puzzle are put together in John 17:23 where Jesus affirms that the Father loved the disciples "even as you [the Father] loved me [Jesus]." This is astounding! Jesus is saying that the Father loves us *just like* or *even as* he loves Jesus! Think for a moment of the magnitude of affection God the Father has for God the Son. That's how much God loves you! Therefore, when John says that our confidence is based on the fact that we are as Jesus is, he means *we are loved by the Father as Jesus is loved by the Father!* No wonder all fear is cast out (1 John 4:18). There is no need to fear him who you know feels only love for you.

But if this is true, how can Paul speak positively and affirmatively in 2 Corinthians 5:11 of "knowing the fear of the Lord"? Had Paul failed to attain for himself a sense of God's love in the way John had? Clearly not, as 2 Corinthians 5:14 attests. How, then, do we resolve this problem? In fact, let me exacerbate things by mentioning other texts that go so far as to *command* fear, such as Luke 12:5; Acts 9:31; Romans 11:20; 2 Corinthians 7:1; Philippians 2:12; and 1 Peter 2:17.

This is not unlike David's remarkable exhortation in Psalm 34:8–9 where he tells us to "taste and see that the LORD is good," an obvious reference to the mercy and love and grace of God, yet follows this immediately with the command that we are to "fear the LORD"!

Do we not, then, truly have a problem? No, we don't, once we recognize that David, Paul, Luke, Peter, and John are all using the word "fear" in two different senses, depending on the context of their comments and even more importantly the differing *judgments* that are in view. But for the sake of time and space, let me restrict my observations to Paul in 2 Corinthians 5 and John in 1 John 4.

A close look at 1 John 4 indicates that the "judgment" to which he refers is punitive. It is the "day" on which the wrath of God against sin and unbelief will be manifest. John is not speaking of godly reverence for Jesus but rather the dread of the criminal who stands guilty in a court of law awaiting sentence. His point, therefore, is that we no longer fear the *punishment* of God as judge (v. 18b) because we know and are assured of the *pleasure* of God as Lord and Lover and Savior of our souls!

This distinction must also be applied in the reading of 2 Corinthians 5:11. As we noted in an earlier meditation, Paul has in mind the fear of loss of reward, not salvation. His fear is awakened and sustained by the realization that he, like all of us, will one day "appear before the judgment seat of Christ" to "receive what is due for what he has done in the body, whether good or evil" (v. 10).

There is a legitimate trembling and discomfiting of the soul in anticipation of the day on which we will give an account for our lives and the opportunities either seized or squandered for Christ. But this has nothing to do with our eternal salvation or God's undying love for us or the status of our souls as forever forgiven through the blood of Christ. In fact, I'm persuaded that it is precisely his love for us as Savior, in *justifying us apart from works*, that instills in our souls a profound, trembling, and deeply awesome respect for Christ as Judge, in *rewarding us according to our works*.

Therefore, the "fear" that John says is inconsistent with "love" is fear of eternal judgment, the fear of enduring the wrath of God for sin, the fear that our guilt has not been forgiven. Entering into the unshakable knowledge and experiential assurance of Christ's "love" for us will, over time, progressively drive from our souls all "fear" of facing a vengeful and angry God. We can, therefore, as John says, "have confidence" on that day of judgment.

On the other hand, the "fear" that Paul says is *consistent* with "love" is the realization that we will yet have to give an account to God for the life that his redeeming love has made possible. Knowing now that one day I will stand before the God whose unending love for me has forever removed all ground for condemnation (Rom. 8:1), while every word and deed are exposed and given their "due" (2 Cor. 5:10) is cause for trembling (but not terror!).

We should, therefore, feel no hesitancy or inconsistency in heeding David's two-fold counsel "to taste and see that the LORD is good" (for "blessed is the man who takes refuge in him"), and to "fear the LORD" (since "those who fear him have no lack") (Ps. 34:8–9).

"Never mind, Houston. Problem solved!"

161

33

Seeing Others Spiritually: A Practical Consequence of the Cross

2 Corinthians 5:16

From now on, therefore, we regard no one according to the flesh. Even though we once regarded Christ according to the flesh, we regard him thus no longer.

W hat is the first thing that comes to mind when you think about the death and resurrection of Christ? I suspect that most would point to such truths as the forgiveness of sins, or the fact that in his death the wrath of God was satisfied, or that we are redeemed and Satan is defeated and heaven is secured. Surely, all these and countless other truths are consequences of what Christ accomplished on our behalf.

But what are the implications of his atoning work for how we relate to *other people?* What are the *horizontal* effects of what he achieved at Calvary? Does the cross have any meaningful influence on how we think of others and how we relate to them?

My reason for asking this question is something Paul said in 2 Corinthians 5:16, a verse often overlooked in favor of the glorious assertion that precedes it in verses 14–15 and the monumental declaration that follows in verse 17. It's all too easy for verse 16 to get lost in the valley, as it were, overshadowed by the towering twin peaks of what comes before and what follows.

In 2 Corinthians 5:14–15 we read of the love of Christ revealed in his death for sinners and their new life in him. In 2 Corinthians 5:17 we are told that because of this remarkable achievement, all who are now "in Christ" are "a new creation" in which the "old" has passed away. A marvelous pair of theological truths indeed! But we dare not ignore the equally profound practical implications that flow from them.

We are alerted to this by the word "therefore" in verse 16. There is obviously a significant conclusion to be drawn from the fact that Christ died for all so that those who live might no longer live for themselves but for Christ who died for them and was raised again.

Christ's redemptive sufferings on Paul's behalf have done far more than simply alter his relationship with God. Yes, his sins are forgiven, and all guilt is washed away. He is justified, adopted, and destined for eternal bliss. But it is also the case that, because of what Christ has achieved in his atoning death, Paul has experienced a radical and far-reaching transformation in his relationship with other people. And so should we.

Paul says that "therefore," because of the love of Christ revealed in his death for me, I no longer regard or evaluate or assess people "according to the flesh" (v. 16). What does the apostle mean by this?

People have interpreted the phrase, "according to the flesh," in countless ways. The consensus today is that it has nothing to do with the so-called *sinful nature* or sensual passions, but rather means "in accordance with the standards and values that derive from living as if physical life in this world is all that exists."[1]

Before his encounter with Christ on the road to Damascus, Paul (then Saul) evaluated other people on the basis of external and worldly standards. Of greatest concern to him were such things as: What is your nationality? Are you a Jew or a Gentile? Are you educated or ignorant? Are you wealthy or poor? Are you male or female? Are you circumcised? Are you "barbarian, Scythian, slave, [or] free" (Col. 3:11).

Let's be honest. We all have our own personal standards of judgment. We unconsciously appeal to certain criteria to evaluate the worth of people in our world. It may be the color of their skin or their financial portfolio. How often do we draw conclusions based on physical attractiveness or style of dress? Other criteria that inform our assessment include such things as political party affiliation, social influence, educational achievement, nobility of birth, bloodline, verbal eloquence, athletic prowess, and the list could go on.

For Paul, perhaps the most important distinction that governed his pre-Christian value system was whether one was a Jew or a Gentile. But the blood of the cross has forever obliterated any spiritual significance in that racial difference (Eph. 2:11–22). While one's ethnicity remains (in that sense I will always be a Gentile and Paul will always be a Jew), it has lost any value in determining one's status with God or place within his kingdom. The only relevant factor is one's relationship with Christ. Indeed, "if *anyone* is *in Christ*," as Paul says in 2 Corinthians 5:17, "he is a new creation. The old has passed away; behold, the new has come." And one critical element of the "old" that has passed away is the appeal to external, worldly, physical, or ethnic standards for determining what is worthy of our devotion or who is qualified to inherit the promises of God.

I want to be perfectly clear. I am an American citizen. I love my country. I cherish my heritage. I am as patriotic as the next guy (perhaps more so). And if the need should arise, I would happily fight in defense of this land and the freedom that it affords. But I have a deeper connection with and a greater commitment to Christians in Russia and Iraq than I do to non-Christians in America. My primary, foundational, and fundamental allegiance is to the universal body of Christ, the church. I am first and foremost a citizen of heaven (Phil. 3:20). My greatest allegiance is to "the city of the living God, the heavenly Jerusalem . . ." (Heb. 12:22), and only secondarily to Washington, DC.

The apostle Paul was born a Jew, "of the tribe of Benjamin, a Hebrew of Hebrews . . ." (Phil. 3:5). But that was of absolutely no importance and carried no weight when it came to his relationship with God or his inheritance within the kingdom of the promises that God had made. All that mattered, Paul said, was whether or not you are "in Christ Jesus" by faith (Gal. 3:26). And "if you are Christ's, then you are Abraham's offspring, heirs according to promise" (Gal. 3:29), regardless of your ethnicity ("Jew or Greek"), your social status ("slave or free"), or your gender ("male or female").

Everything must now be viewed in light of the "new creation" that has come with the redemptive work and resurrection life of Christ! Conversion for each of us entails a radically transformed standard for assessing what is valuable and true and deserving of our allegiance and sacrifice.

In the second half of verse 16 Paul extends this principle to his relationship with Christ himself. "Even though we once regarded Christ according to the flesh," Paul says, "we regard him thus no longer" (v. 16).

Did Paul know of Jesus prior to his conversion? Certainly he had heard of him. Jesus spent considerable time in Jerusalem during his years of public ministry, as did the young rabbi, Saul of Tarsus. Whether or not he met him personally prior to his Damascus Road experience is not stated (but is doubtful, in my opinion). But verse 16 has nothing to do with whether Paul had personal knowledge of Jesus during his earthly life or whether he was interested in the historical facts concerning Jesus' existence in Palestine. Nor is Paul referring to knowing "Jesus" in his humanity as over against knowing him in his exalted and supernatural status as risen "Christ."

Rather, here (v. 16b) Paul is repudiating his pre-Christian evaluation of Jesus. Before conversion he saw him as a blasphemer, a "misguided messianic pretender, [and] a crucified heretic."[2] He now sees him as the Son of God in human flesh whose death on a cross is the power of God unto salvation.

To what extent do worldly or merely human standards still govern and shape how you evaluate other people? What criteria do you employ: ethnic, financial, and physical, or spiritual, biblical, and moral? Whom do you admire: the self-centered, "successful" reprobate or the humble and rarely recognized servant of others? Why are you attracted to them (or, conversely, repulsed): is it the color of their skin or the character of their soul? What matters most: the flag that flies over their country or the faith that resides in their heart?

If you are "in Christ," then all things are new (v. 17), including how you think, feel, and will, as well as the basis on which you judge, assess, and evaluate. May the truth of the cross and the principles of the Spirit govern our perspective on others, rather than the warped ways of this fallen world.

34

Behold! A New Creation!

2 Corinthians 5:17

Therefore, if anyone is in Christ, he is a new creation. The old has passed away; behold, the new has come.

Few things are more frustrating than the gradual erosion of meaning in Christian language. For example, I often wonder if the people who applaud the hymn "Amazing Grace" have any idea of what they are singing. Do they know what it means, biblically speaking, to be a "lost" "wretch" in need of "salvation"? Sadly, the notion of divine "grace" that redeems from sin and delivers from eternal wrath, apart from human works, has been domesticated, secularized, and emptied of its theological significance.

Much the same is true of being "born again." Those who claim to have experienced the "new birth" often equate it with the regret they feel for their most recent DUI or arrest for drug possession. When faced with public reproach and possible jail time, professional athletes and morally stunted pop culture icons find it useful to affirm they've "found God" through some ill-defined "new birth" religious encounter.

How far and away different that is from the imagery Paul employs in 2 Corinthians 5:17.

167

Although he doesn't use the terminology of being "born again," Paul surely has in view the same concept as Jesus (John 3:3–8), Peter (1 Pet. 1:23), and John (1 John 2:29; 3:9; 5:1) when he speaks of a "new creation" for those who are "in Christ" (2 Cor. 5:17).

There is a strong likelihood that Paul's language here of a "new creation" is also an allusion to the "new heaven and new earth" of Revelation 21–22. If so, his point would be that our experience of the new birth is a personal prelude to the corporate and cosmic dimensions of the new creation that will come when Christ does. Simply put, the glory of the age to come has impinged upon or broken into the present. *We are reborn microcosms of the eschatological macrocosm!*

That being said, we can't escape the individual and personal focus that Paul has in view in this text, as seen in his emphasis on "anyone" who is "in Christ" being a new creation. Earlier in 2 Corinthians 4:6 Paul portrayed the conversion experience as a creative act of God comparable to the original creation of light out of darkness. Here he returns to that theme with added emphasis on the transformed nature and newness of the person who is the object of his saving action.

This "new creation" or "new birth" or "regeneration" (see Titus 3:5) or being "born again" does not mean merely the mending of one's ways, the changing of bad habits, or embracing a new list of do's and don'ts. It refers to a radical, pervasive spiritual re-creation of the inner being.

No wonder Paul calls for our undivided attentiveness to this glorious truth with the declarative, "behold." Be stunned, be very stunned! That you are an utterly new creation, the spiritual product of the gracious and life-giving power of God, is a breathtaking reality. Behold! Stop and consider this remarkable and triumphant truth. Don't pass it by with only a casual glance. Give it the focus it is due. Behold!

Could it be that many Christians struggle and languish because they fail to grasp the far reaching and spiritually radical implications of being a "new creation"? Could it be that some of you live unnecessarily enslaved to "old things," because the truth of verse 17 has never been given the weight it ought to bear? That's right, *unneces-*

sarily enslaved. You need not live in bondage to "old things," be they stubborn habits or deceptive values or destructive relationships or wrong-headed beliefs. The God who was kind enough and strong enough to create you anew is equally committed to supplying you with the resources and energy to live consistently with what you are. You are now "in Christ"! You are now "a new creation"!

What are the "old things" that hold you back and keep you down? Are you still beholden to false beliefs about your personal identity? Have you failed to realize that you are a child of God, not of Satan, and are adopted into his family, destined to reign with Christ as a coheir in the kingdom of heaven? Have you failed to realize that you are reckoned as righteous in God's sight, fully and forever forgiven of all your sins, sealed and filled with the Spirit of promise and power?

The "old" things have passed away. So stop living as if they had any claim on your life. "New things" have come: a new covenant (Luke 22:20; Heb. 8:8), a new creation (Gal. 6:15), a new humanity (Eph. 2:15), a new name (Rev. 2:17; 3:12), a new city (Rev. 3:12; 21:2), as well as a new standing, a new power, a new hope, and a new destiny. Resist the temptation to reduce being born again to a momentary existential crisis or a convenient religious enlightenment, neither of which yields the fruit of the Holy Spirit and a passionate pursuit of Jesus Christ and his glory in all things. Behold! If you are truly in Christ you are a new creation. Behold!

There is no escaping the fact that Paul has in view a complete and pervasive restructuring of your life, your values, and your agenda for the future, as well as your identity as a redeemed image-bearer. The conditions, relationships, worldly perspectives, and carnal principles that once dominated your life are the "old things" that have "passed away." All thinking and willing and feeling and judging are now governed by a new and undying power.

Don't embrace the pernicious lie that life will never change or that sinful circumstances will always dominate your existence. The enemy would have you believe that spiritual growth is an elusive dream and the future is a dark and endless repetition of past failures. To that, Paul would say to you in no uncertain terms, "*Behold!* If you are in Christ you are a *new creation!*"

I'm not advocating a "power of positive thinking" approach to life, as if by merely willing yourself to believe the best that all of life will automatically change. Don't mistake my exhortation for the gushing, semireligious, feel-good nonsense that certain (here to remain unnamed) preachers deliver monotonously each week to millions of gullible viewers. I'm speaking about the grace-grounded, blood-bought power of a new life in Christ that enables you to embrace with joy the forgiveness of sins and to welcome with a cross-centered confidence the trials and sufferings that will inevitably come your way.

Countless Internet ads, roadside billboards, radio advertisements, and more than a few deceptive TV evangelists compete for your attention every moment of the day, promising you an enticing but ultimately false future (for a small fee, of course, or a "seed-faith" donation to the "ministry") that will supposedly enable you to escape the rut of your past and present.

Don't believe them! There is only one voice and one glorious truth worthy of your faith. "*Behold!* Take note of this one, marvelous truth! If you are in Christ, you are a *new creation*. The old, by the mercy of Christ, has passed away. The new, because of the cross of Christ, has come!"

35

When God Saves Sinners from God

2 Corinthians 5:18–21

All this is from God, who through Christ reconciled us to himself and gave us the ministry of reconciliation; that is, in Christ God was reconciling the world to himself, not counting their trespasses against them, and entrusting to us the message of reconciliation. Therefore, we are ambassadors for Christ, God making his appeal through us. We implore you on behalf of Christ, be reconciled to God. For our sake he made him to be sin who knew no sin, so that in him we might become the righteousness of God.

If asked for a concise, biblical definition of the gospel, indeed, a definition of Christianity itself, one could hardly be faulted for pointing to 2 Corinthians 5:18–21.

One could (and probably should) spend weeks in this text. It is a rich and wide-ranging treasure house of theological truth. But the more I think about it, the more I'm convinced that the brief comments of James Denney will suffice. After reading them, I strongly suspect you'll agree. So, I ask that you do more than merely read his words (please, for your own sake, don't skip over them). Meditate

171

on the profound implications of what he says. I'll interject a few relevant comments along the way.

Denney begins with a question, the answer to which is foundational to understanding the core of Christianity:

> What is it that makes a Gospel necessary? What is it that the wisdom and love of God undertake to deal with, and do deal with, in that marvelous way which constitutes the Gospel? Is it man's distrust of God? Is it man's dislike, fear, antipathy, spiritual alienation? Not if we accept the Apostle's teaching. The serious thing which makes the Gospel necessary, and the putting away of which constitutes the Gospel, is God's condemnation of the world and its sin; it is God's wrath, "revealed from heaven against all ungodliness and unrighteousness of men" (Rom. 1:16–18). The putting away of this is "reconciliation"; the preaching of *this* reconciliation is the preaching of the Gospel.[1]

Here Denney touches on something rarely considered by most Christians. Let me put it in slightly different terms. *From what is it that we need to be saved?* Certainly not "from ourselves" (although one often hears such language, even in the church). Most Christians would say, "from hell." In a sense, they are correct. But why is hell a threat, and what is it that accounts for the existence of hell and the experience of those who end up there?

The answer, as Denney points out, is divine *wrath*. Our only hope is for God to save us from God! This is the great glory of the gospel, that God in his grace takes action in Christ to save us from God in his wrath. God is not pitted against himself in this marvelous act of mercy, for God *honors* God when his love makes provision to satisfy the demands of his wrath.

Divine justice and its expression in divine wrath against sin, to use Paul's words, calls for the reckoning or "counting" of our trespasses "against" us (2 Cor. 5:19). So how is it that, instead, I am forgiven the guilt of these wicked deeds? The apostle's answer, in verse 21, is that God "made him [Jesus] to be sin who knew no sin, so that in him we might become the righteousness of God." Don't ever think that the love of God means that the wrath of God was ignored. Because God is just and righteous, there must be a reckoning or "counting" of trespasses. But because God is loving and gracious, the "counting" or "imputing" and the punishment it entailed fell on Christ.

I've often said to people that the reason why the psalmist declares that God "does not deal with *us* according to our sins . . ." (Ps. 103:10) is because God dealt with *Jesus* according to our sins! Grace and mercy do not mean that sin is not dealt with, as if to suggest God merely swept our sins under the carpet of his compassion and ignored the horrid offense of our rebellion. Far from it! God the Father "counted" our trespasses against God the Son and in doing so brought about the reconciliation.

This "counting" or "reckoning" of our sins against him is what he means in verse 21 when he speaks of Jesus being "made to be sin" on our behalf. Paul is talking about the liability to suffer the penal consequences of the law. Our guilt, incurred because of our trespasses, has been imputed to Christ so that we, through faith in his sufferings on our behalf, might have his righteousness imputed to us!

We must not overlook the fact that all this was achieved by him who "knew no sin." That *as God* he is without sin goes without saying, "but what is of vital importance for us and our reconciliation is that *as Man*, that is, in His incarnate state, Christ knew no sin, for only on that ground was He qualified to effect an atonement as Man for man."[2]

Now, back to Denney:

When St. Paul says that God has given him the ministry of reconciliation, he means that he is a preacher of this peace. He ministers reconciliation to the world. . . . It is not the main part of his vocation to tell men to make their peace with God, but to tell them that God has made peace with the world. At bottom, the Gospel is not good advice, but good news. All the good advice it gives is summed up in this—Receive the good news. But if the good news be taken away; if we cannot say, God has made peace, God has dealt seriously with His condemnation of sin, so that it no longer stands in the way of your return to Him; if we cannot say, Here *is* the reconciliation, receive it,—then for man's actual state we have no Gospel at all. . . .

When Christ's work was done, the reconciliation of the world was accomplished. When men were called to receive it, they were called to a relation to God, not in which they would no more be against Him—though that is included—but in which they would no more have Him against them. There would be no condemnation thenceforth to those who were in Christ Jesus.[3]

Becoming the "righteousness of God" (v. 21) is not simply a tall order, but an impossible one. Yet, there he says it: in Christ Jesus we have "become the righteousness of God"!

Theologian Richard Hooker said that as inconceivable as it may seem, from a human point of view, "such we are in the sight of God the Father as is the very Son of God himself. Let it be counted folly or frenzy or fury or whatever. It is our wisdom and our comfort; we care for no knowledge in the world but this: *that man hath sinned and God hath suffered; that God hath made himself the sin of men, and that men are made the righteousness of God.*"

What a glorious gospel indeed!

Could Jesus Have Sinned?

2 Corinthians 5:21

For our sake he made him to be sin who knew no sin, so that in him we might become the righteousness of God.

I "know" sin. I say this not because I can define sin, although I can. I say this not because I can identify sin when I see it, although I can also do that. I say it because I am a sinner. I "know" sin because I commit it, sadly, on a daily basis. My acquaintance with sin, therefore, does not come from associating with others who transgress or from reading a book on *hamartiology* (the technical, theological term for the study of sin). I "know" sin, because I, like David, was "brought forth in iniquity, and in sin did my mother conceive me" (Ps. 51:5). I "know" sin because I sin.

Jesus, on the other hand, "knew no sin" (2 Cor. 5:21). Again, the apostle Paul doesn't mean by this that Jesus was unaware of the existence of sin or that he lived in isolation from those who commit sin. He was not intellectually ignorant of sin or unacquainted with its devastating consequences. He "knew no sin" in the sense that he never personally committed one. He was sinless.

How often do we pause and give thanks for the sinlessness of Christ? Were he not sinless, the entire scheme of reconciliation that

Paul outlines in 2 Corinthians 5:18–21 would fall flat on its face. The glorious and gracious work of God in reconciling the world to himself hinges on God "not counting" our trespasses against us because he has counted our trespasses against Christ. But this would be to no avail if Christ himself had committed trespasses that ought to have been "counted" against him. The reckoning or imputing of our guilt to Jesus, for which he then suffers the wrath of God in our stead, is only redemptive if he is himself personally guilt free.

The New Testament is crystal clear on this point. Although 2 Corinthians 5:21 is the only explicit affirmation of Christ's sinlessness in Paul's writings, we should also take note of his reference to the "obedience" of the Son in both Romans 5:19 and Philippians 2:8.

Jesus gave the religious leaders of his day every opportunity to identify some sin in his life. "Which one of you convicts me of sin?" he asked them in public (John 8:46). The author of Hebrews reminds us that "we do not have a high priest who is unable to sympathize with our weaknesses, but one who in every respect has been tempted as we are, *yet without sin*" (Heb. 4:15). Jesus, he later tells us, was "holy, innocent, [and] unstained" (Heb. 7:26). He was "a lamb without blemish or spot" (1 Pet. 1:19) and "committed no sin" (1 Pet. 2:22).

That he *didn't* sin is a settled and undeniable fact. But *could* he have sinned? Was it in any way a *possibility* for him to have sinned or was it in every way impossible that he should ever have transgressed? Or, to use theological terms, was Jesus *impeccable* (incapable of sinning), or *peccable* (capable of sinning, although remaining sinless)?

I intentionally avoid technical theological language in these meditations, but bear with me for a moment as I appeal to four Latin phrases that shed light on this issue. The first is *non posse non peccare*, which means "not able not to sin." This describes unregenerate people and the fallen angels (i.e., demons). In other words, they necessarily sin.

Two other phrases are *posse peccare* ("able to sin") and *posse non peccare* ("able not to sin"). These describe Adam before the fall, regenerate people, and Jesus, if one denies his impeccability. Finally, there is *non posse peccare*, or "not able to sin." This would be true of God, the saints in heaven, and Jesus, if one affirms his impeccability.

My question is this: Was Jesus Christ sinless because he *could* not sin (*non posse peccare*) or because he *would* not sin? Was he constitutionally *incapable* of sinning or merely volitionally *unwilling* to sin? To say that Jesus could have sinned, even though he did not, is to say he was *peccable*. To say that Jesus could not have sinned, and therefore didn't, is to say he was *impeccable*.

The most helpful concrete illustration of this issue is the confrontation Jesus had with Satan in the wilderness (Luke 4:1–13). When Satan came to him with those three temptations, *could* Jesus have succumbed? We know he didn't, and we are eternally grateful. But was it *possible* for him *not* to have resisted? Those who affirm impeccability respond with a definitive "no"! Those who deny impeccability counter with three observations, only two of which, in my opinion, are helpful.

First, those who deny impeccability argue that if he could not sin, he was not truly human. After all, "to err is human." This argument is weak, for it is not necessary to human nature that one be capable of sinning. When finally in heaven, having been glorified, the saints will be incapable of sinning, but they will not for that reason be less human then than they are now on earth.

A second argument often heard is that if Jesus could not have sinned, he was not genuinely tempted. True temptation requires the possibility of sinning. That he refused to yield to Satan's temptations no one denies. But yielding must have been *possible* or the encounter was a sham.

Some respond by saying that perhaps *Jesus didn't know* he was impeccable. In other words, even though he couldn't yield to temptation, he was unaware of the impossibility. Therefore, at least so far as his own conscious experience is concerned, the temptation would have been quite genuine. But I find it hard to believe that Jesus lacked such self-awareness. Even if he did, we don't, so what benefit is there to us in his having resisted the Devil's overtures? In other words, we find encouragement in Jesus' example only if we know he could have sinned, but didn't (1 Pet. 2:21–23). So long as *we* know that his sinning was absolutely impossible, the force of his example is undermined, regardless of what *he* may have known.

A third and final argument by those who deny impeccability is that the doctrine is based on the belief that Jesus resisted the Devil from the strength of his divine nature. Satan was tempting God and God, by definition, cannot sin. Regardless of the strength of his seductive appeals, Satan didn't stand a chance. After all, the finite cannot conquer the infinite. The presence within the incarnate second person of the Godhead of a holy and omnipotent divine nature made it impossible for him to have yielded to Satan's overtures.

For many years I strongly advocated the impeccability of Christ, insisting that because he was *God* incarnate he was incapable of sinning. Now, make no mistake, he was and forever is God incarnate. But I'm not so sure about his impeccability, and here's why.

As I have argued extensively elsewhere, I believe Jesus lived and ministered as a *human, dependent on the power of the Holy Spirit.*[1] As a human, the possibility existed that he *could* have sinned, but by virtue of his unceasing reliance on the power of the Holy Spirit he *did not* sin. Like the first Adam, Jesus could have sinned. But as the second Adam, he chose not to.

This means that in becoming a man "the Son of God willed to renounce the exercise of his divine powers, attributes, prerogatives, so that he might live fully within those limitations which inhere in being truly human."[2] That which he had (all the divine attributes), by virtue of what he was (the second person of the Trinity), he willingly chose not to use. Thus we see a human being doing superhuman things and ask, "How?" The answer is: Not from the power of his own divine nature, but through the power of the Holy Spirit.

Thus the Son chose to experience the world through the limitations imposed by human consciousness and an authentic human nature. The attributes of omnipotence, omnipresence, and omniscience were not lost or laid aside, but became *latent* and *potential* within the confines of his human nature. They are present in Jesus in all their fullness, but they are no longer in conscious exercise. The incarnation thus means that Jesus "actually thought and acted, viewed the world, and experienced time and space events strictly within the confines of a normally developing human person."[3]

Look again at the various accounts of Jesus' temptation by Satan. We are told that he was not only led *into* the wilderness by the Spirit (Matt. 4:1) but was also being led by the Spirit *in* the wilderness during the entire course of the forty days (Luke 4:1; it was, no doubt, the Spirit who led Jesus to fast). "If he was being tempted by Satan for forty days (Mark 1:13), he was being led by the Spirit for those same forty days (Luke 4:1). It is impossible to escape the conclusion that these Gospel writers want their readers to understand that Jesus met and conquered the usurping enemy of God not by his own power alone but was aided in his victory by the power of the Holy Spirit."[4] He was fortified and energized by the continual infusion of divine power from the Spirit of God (see John 3:34).

If someone should ask, "But why or how did the human Jesus *always* choose to rely on the power of the Spirit and thereby not sin?" The answer would be that the Spirit was always antecedent to any choice that Jesus was to make, enabling and energizing him to continue in his conscious reliance on the power the Spirit was providing. Is that not also the case with us? To whatever degree and however frequently we choose not to sin, it is because the Spirit antecedently empowered us to choose to avail ourselves of his presence and supply.

It could conceivably be said, therefore, that Jesus was *peccable* when it came to the *metaphysical potential* for sin in his own human nature (in other words, there was nothing inherent within the person of Christ that made it impossible for him to sin, any more than it was so in the case of Adam), but *impeccable* insofar as it was impossible for the Spirit to fail to energize Jesus' will to depend upon the power that the Spirit supplied.

The implications of this for you and me are profound, and I defer, in conclusion, to the words of Gerald Hawthorne to make the point:

> Not only is Jesus their Savior because of who he was and because of his own complete obedience to the Father's will (cf. Heb. 10:5–7), but he is the supreme example for them of what is possible in a human life because of his own total dependence upon the Spirit of God. Jesus is living proof of how those who are his followers may exceed the limitations of their humanness in order that they, like him, might carry to completion against all odds their God-given mission in life—

179

by the Holy Spirit. Jesus demonstrated clearly that God's intended way for human beings to live, the ideal way to live, the supremely successful way to live, is in conjunction with God, in harmony with God, in touch with the power of God, and not apart from God, not independent of God, not without God. The Spirit was the presence and power of God in Jesus, and fully so.[5]

Receiving the Grace
of God in Vain

2 Corinthians 6:1–2

Working together with him, then, we appeal to you not to
receive the grace of God in vain. For he says,

> "In a favorable time I listened to you,
> and in a day of salvation I have helped you."

Behold, now is the favorable time; behold, now is the day of
salvation.

I struggle to think of a more glowing endorsement than that which
Paul gave the church in Thessalonica. He applauds them for the
fact that when the gospel was preached they "received the word
in much affliction, with the joy of the Holy Spirit" (1 Thess. 1:6).
Again, "when you received the word of God, which you heard from
us, you accepted it not as the word of men but as what it really is,
the word of God, which is at work in you believers" (1 Thess. 2:13).
Needless to say, no one would ever suggest that the Thessalonians
had received the grace of God "in vain"!

Sadly, the same can't be said of everyone. We see that from 2 Corinthians 6:1–2.

What does Paul mean by "the grace of God"? And what does it mean to "receive" it "in vain"?

The first question is the easier of the two. It may be that "the grace of God" is simply Paul's shorthand way of referring to the gospel and its benefits. In light of the immediately preceding context, he may have specifically in mind the new attitude of 5:16, the new creation of 5:17, the reconciliation of 5:18–19, or the righteousness of God of 5:21. All of this is wrapped up in the word "salvation" in 2 Corinthians 6:2. Murray Harris is correct in pointing out that "within the wider context of the letter, 'the grace of God' will also refer to the present opportunity that the Corinthians have to become fully reconciled to Paul."[1]

The second question, obviously, is more difficult to answer. Some believe he is urging them not to forfeit the grace of salvation that they had earlier received. In other words, Paul exhorts them to persevere and to avoid apostasy.

Others suggest that the exhortation in verses 1–2 is not directed to those Corinthians who are already born again, but to those in Corinth who had repeatedly heard the gospel but had made no decision. Paul was not so naïve to think that everyone in the *professing* church was necessarily truly converted. Therefore, his command not to receive the grace of God in vain is equivalent to an exhortation to all men not to reject the gospel of Jesus Christ. But is "to receive in vain" really the same as to utterly "reject"? I don't think so, as I'll point out below.

God's grace may be received in vain when it is received superficially or externally, as in the parable of the soils (Luke 8:4–15; Matt. 13:18–23). There the seed (gospel) falls upon rocky ground or among thorns, to be snatched away or choked by the temptations of this world. This view is similar to the previous one, insofar as the people in view are unbelievers. The difference is that, according to this interpretation, people don't explicitly reject the gospel but "receive" and "believe" it, but only in a superficial way. Their so-called "faith" is spurious and therefore temporary.

Perhaps receiving the grace of God in vain pertains not so much to salvation per se, or its forfeiture, but to the loss of potential blessings related to spiritual growth, knowledge, and joy that the Corinthians would suffer by rejecting Paul as their apostle. In other words, the people are truly saved. They have genuinely received the gospel and believed it, but they have failed to progress in their Christian growth and stand in danger of losing those spiritual blessings and rewards they otherwise might have obtained. Philip Hughes embraces a similar view and suggests that

> for them to receive the grace of God in vain meant that their practice did not measure up to their profession as Christians, that their lives were so inconsistent as to constitute a denial of the logical implications of the gospel, namely, and in particular, that Christ died for them so that they might no longer live to themselves but to His glory.[2]

In other words, the passionate conviction that accompanied their salvation had not as yet performed its transforming work in their lives. It is to that progressive transformation of their daily experience that Paul is urging and exhorting them.

Judith Gundry Volf suggests that to receive the grace of God in vain may be referring largely, if not exclusively, to their opposition to the apostle himself. The context surrounding this statement is Paul's description of his ministry on their behalf and his attempt to restore good relations with the Corinthians (2 Cor. 5:13–14; 5:18–6:1; see esp. his impassioned appeal in 6:11–13). In Paul's opinion, to reject *him* is to reject the divine grace of which he is a minister. Volf then argues that Paul's appeal is simply *"for the sake of argument only."*[3] That is, he does not believe they *will* reject or deny him, but if they were to do so it would be tantamount to receiving the grace of God, which was his message to them, in vain.

I think the key to this difficult text is found in the word translated "vain" (*kenos*; see also its use in Gal. 2:2; Phil. 2:16; and 1 Thess. 3:5). It typically means either "empty" or without content or, as here, "vain" or *without purpose or result*. Harris argues that "to receive God's grace 'in vain' (*eis kenon*) is not to 'reject' it . . . or even to 'neglect' it . . . but to receive it without profit, without the intended effect being achieved. The grace is accepted, but it never attains its goal; it comes to nothing."[4] If so, "Paul is exhorting his Corinthian converts not to fail to profit from the proffered divine grace, or, expressed positively, to give God's grace an effective welcome, to capitalize on opportunities for spiritual growth."[5]

But how might they let God's grace come to no end?

Consider Paul's exhortation to the Colossians that they conduct themselves wisely "toward outsiders, making the best use of the time" (Col. 4:5) or "making the most of the opportunity." Similarly, if the Corinthians "squandered God-given opportunities for bringing spiritual benefit to themselves and to unbelievers . . . and if they failed to exercise the ministry of reconciliation (5:18) and to fulfill their role as Christ's ambassadors (5:19); more specifically, if they accommodated the false apostles (11:13–15), or embraced a 'different gospel' (11:4), or failed to repudiate paganism (6:14–18) and personal sin (7:1; 12:20–21), or spurned Paul's overtures of reconciliation (6:13; 7:2),"[6] they would be guilty of having received the grace of God "in vain."

If this view is correct, and I'm inclined to think it is, Paul's appeal is to Christians that they avail themselves of God's gracious enabling so that the purpose or aim of their salvation might be attained. The "grace of God" is designed to equip believers to proclaim Christ and not themselves (2 Cor. 4:5) and to live for Christ and not themselves (see 5:15). I also agree with Harris that "if God's grace flows continuously, a single failure to benefit from it would not stem the flow. What would be compromised, however, would be the receipt of commendatory recompense at Christ's tribunal (5:10)."[7]

To receive the grace of God in vain, therefore, is not to reject it altogether and live as an unbeliever, nor is it to receive the grace of God and subsequently forfeit or lose its saving power. Rather, Paul is talking about the urgency and importance of the Corinthians responding to God's grace in humble obedience and seizing every opportunity to "please" the Lord (2 Cor. 5:9) in how they live, speak, act, and perhaps especially in how they respond to his efforts to rebuild and restore a relationship that had been undermined by suspicion, false reports, and the sinister efforts of the false teachers in their city.

God's grace comes to us not simply once in the gospel but as a constant and never-ceasing flow of merciful enablement and sanctifying power. Like the Corinthians, we must be diligent to avail ourselves of it at all times, taking advantage of every occasion to do "good" (rather than "evil") so that it might attain to the goal for which God has bestowed it and so that we might receive "what is due" for what we, by means of that very grace, have "done in the body" (see 2 Cor. 5:10).

38

The Most Eloquent
Advertisement for the Gospel

2 Corinthians 6:3

We put no obstacle in anyone's way, so that no fault may be found with our ministry.

enator Charles Grassley of Iowa, the ranking Republican on the Senate Finance Committee, made news by announcing his intention to investigate several prominent Christian ministries to determine whether they have exploited their tax-exempt status as churches to provide themselves with opulent and lavish lifestyles. Those who've been asked by the Senator to submit financial records include Benny Hinn, Kenneth Copeland, Creflo Dollar, Joyce Meyer, Eddie Long, and Paula White.

Without intending to pass premature judgment on these individuals, Senator Grassley's action is indicative of a belief that exists among most people, both Christian and non-Christian, that the *conduct* of a "minister" ought to be consistent with the *content* of his or her "message." Grassley evidently shares the opinion of many who believe that the church and its ministry are discredited by the disreputable behavior of its leaders and members. Conversely, the mes-

186

sage can be enhanced and adorned by the godliness, humility, and self-sacrifice of those who proclaim the gospel of Christ crucified.

Whether or not these particular leaders are living in a way that undermines the message or in some way brings reproach on the name of Christ is for each person to decide. But the fact remains that how we as Christians conduct ourselves in the sight of others has massive repercussions on their assessment of the gospel we preach.

No one knew this better than the apostle Paul. In fact, most of 2 Corinthians is concerned with his conduct as a gospel minister and whether or not it condemns or commends him as a genuine apostle of Jesus Christ. Second Corinthians 6:3–10 is perhaps the most explicit example of this in the entire book. We will spend several meditations unpacking its rich and instructive content. Here is what Paul said:

> We put no obstacle in anyone's way, so that no fault may be found with our ministry, but as servants of God we commend ourselves in every way: by great endurance, in afflictions, hardships, calamities, beatings, imprisonments, riots, labors, sleepless nights, hunger; by purity, knowledge, patience, kindness, the Holy Spirit, genuine love; by truthful speech, and the power of God; with the weapons of righteousness for the right hand and for the left; through honor and dishonor, through slander and praise. We are treated as impostors, and yet are true; as unknown, and yet well known; as dying, and behold, we live; as punished, and yet not killed; as sorrowful, yet always rejoicing; as poor, yet making many rich; as having nothing, yet possessing everything. (2 Cor. 6:3–10)

My concern in this meditation is solely with verse 3. Although the ESV translates the verb simply as "we put," the present tense of the Greek should probably be rendered something along the lines of "we are trying to put no obstacle in anyone's way" with the emphasis on Paul's customary and repeated *modus operandi*. This is the consistent and committed posture of his labors as an apostle. There simply are no circumstances under which Paul would act any other way. There is *never, ever* an excuse for speaking or ministering in such a fashion that "fault" may be found with the good news of eternal life in Jesus Christ.

Paul's preeminent concern is with the "ministry" God has entrusted to him, not his own reputation or position or influence. The only self-commendation he cares for is as a "servant/minister" of God. He is more than willing to be slandered and ridiculed, beaten and imprisoned, just so long as the glorious good news of Christ crucified suffers no reproach.

The word translated to find "fault" (ESV) or be "discredited" (NASB) is a verb related to the noun *momus*, a name given to the Greek god of ridicule or mockery. Paul wants nothing in his life to be used by others as an excuse for laughing at the truth. If offense is to be taken at the gospel, let it be because of the *content* of what he proclaims and not any misconduct in his own life.

The "obstacle" or cause for offense is any questionable action or self-serving speech that would prompt people to doubt Paul's integrity or sincerity and thereby bring the gospel he proclaimed into disrepute or cause it to be ridiculed or censured. In the immediate context, in relation to the Corinthians, Paul might have in mind anything on his part that would hinder their acceptance of him, their fellowship with one another, or their commitment to proclaim and advance the message of the gospel.

Of course, there is no guarantee that in conducting himself properly and in purity that Paul (or we) will avoid the condemnation of others. "He is thinking of *unnecessary* offense and *unjustified* censure."[1] The notion that eternal life is available only by faith in a crucified and risen Messiah is inherently foolish "to those who are perishing" (1 Cor. 1:18). The Jews in Paul's day found it to be a "stumbling block" and the Gentiles mocked it as "foolishness" (1 Cor. 1:23). But where Paul was able to avoid putting an obstacle in anyone's path, he was committed to being scrupulously careful.

To illustrate Paul's point, consider this hypothetical conversation between a Christian ("Steve") and his unbelieving coworker ("Mike").

Steve: "Mike, did you have an opportunity to read that book I gave you about Christianity?"

Mike: "Yes, and I have to be honest in saying that I was offended by much of what it said. I don't particularly like being told I'm morally depraved and a sinner! That's not the sort of language that 'wins friends and influences people'! It's a 'PC world,' Steve, and people don't want to hear it."

Steve: "You're right. They don't. But what they want isn't of paramount importance. What they *need* is the truth, even if it hurts or causes offense. By the way, what was your impression of what the author said about Jesus Christ?"

Mike: "Honestly, I found it a bit ridiculous. That there is only one God who became a human being named Jesus is one thing. But to tell me that he lived a perfect life, died on a cross where he suffered for the sins of people like me, and then came back to life again—well, I felt like I was back in my college course on Greek mythology! Worst of all, though, is the argument that I need to 'repent' of my sins and put my faith in this Jesus as my only hope for reconciliation with God. How absurd! How arrogant of you people!"

Steve: "I understand your reaction, Mike. Really, I do. But I want you to know that I'm praying for you, asking that the Spirit of God will give you eyes to see the beauty in what you now find ugly as well as a new spiritual taste for what you now find bitter. But let me ask you one more thing. Have I behaved in an offensive way? Do you see in me any hypocrisy or insincerity, or do my words or actions come across as incompatible with what you know about Christianity? If so, I need to change."

Mike: "No, my beef isn't with you. Your life is remarkably consistent with your message. I wish I could say that of everyone I've known who called themselves Christians. But I can't."

Steve: "I appreciate that, Mike. But you should know that if there's anything 'good' in me it's all because of the grace of God."

Mike: "See, that's just what I mean. I compliment you, and you're so darn humble! That's a rare thing these days. In fact, if there's anything that makes me want to read the book again and at least think about the claims of Christ, it's the way you're so unashamed about your faith and your love for God. You seem so content, and I've never heard you make a sexual comment about the girls in the office. Yeah, maybe I'll read it again and we can get together and talk about it."

Although not apostles, you and I are "servants of God" and have a "ministry" no less so than Paul. What "obstacles" do we put in the way of others seeing the glory of God revealed in the face of Jesus Christ? Do they find "fault" with your life? Or are they, like Mike, curious about why you turn from immorality and delight in marital fidelity? Are they intrigued by your passion for the beauty of God and your disdain for the tawdry and unseemly trivialities of this world?

When they speak of you behind your back, do they marvel at your contentment or mock you for joining others in fudging on your time sheet? Is it obvious, in the way you talk and work and live, that your happiness is rooted in a transcendent power that cannot be explained in mere earthly terms? To live in such a way that God looks good is costly. Treasuring him above all may not comport well with the ambitious and materialistic ethos of our day. But it pays a rich and eternal reward.

Let us never forget that the gospel itself is more than sufficient to offend self-centered and arrogant sinners. May it never be that we aggravate this effect with our boorish and self-aggrandizing behavior. "It is always true," writes Murray Harris, "that *the life of the Christian is the most eloquent advertisement for the gospel.*"[2]

When People See You, Does God Look Good?

2 Corinthians 6:4

> But as servants of God we commend ourselves in every way:
> by great endurance, in afflictions, hardships, calamities.

In case you skipped it, let me repeat the question in the title: "When people see *you*, does *God* look good?" Not many of us phrase it in precisely that way or even think in those terms. It's far more natural for us to ask, "When people see me, do *I* look good?" Do I impress them with my charisma? Are they captivated by my wit? Are they attracted by how I dress? Did they take note of my intelligence? Do they still think of me an hour or two later?

We are obsessed with what others think of us. We are elated when they find in us something to praise and are crushed when they are offended. That is why we are so given to self-commendation, self-promotion, and self-improvement. So often our very identity and thus our value hang suspended on the opinion of those who "see" us.

But wait a minute. If this sort of concern for self is so sinful, why did Paul "commend" himself to the Corinthians here in 2 Corinthians 6:4? And doesn't this conflict with his earlier denunciation of self-commendation in 3:1? It would appear from these two texts that there are at least two sorts of self-commendation, one good (6:4) and the other bad (3:1).

Let's take a closer look at this passage (6:4), for Paul does not "commend" himself and leave it at that, as if his efforts were devoted to securing a positive response from the Corinthian church. It is as "servants of God," or more accurately, "ministers" of God, that he and his coworkers labor to elicit their approval. And the criteria to which he appeals as grounds for their acceptance are not very appealing: afflictions, hardships, calamities, beatings, imprisonments, hunger, slander, sorrow, and so forth. Not the sort of things one would typically include on a resume!

Evidently Paul believed that commending oneself as a *minister of God* was not only permissible, but mandatory, even godly. How so? What does it mean to draw attention to oneself as a minister of God, and how does it avoid the sinful self-serving that Paul and other biblical writers so consistently condemn?

I want to suggest that commending oneself as a minister of God consists of living and acting and speaking in such a way that others think not of you but of him. They don't so much look *to* you as *through* you, and in the light of your life see him. Again, to use the words of the chapter title, it means conducting yourself in such a manner that when others see you, God looks good. Let me explain this by asking a series of pointed (and painful) questions.

When you pray, do people comment on your eloquence or God's excellency?

When you intercede in a corporate gathering, are those present impressed with your godliness or God's goodness?

On those occasions when your life is subject to public scrutiny, do people think of the heights of your abundance or the depths of your need? Are they inclined to think about your devotion and how fortunate God is to have you as his "minister," or are they awakened to your utter dependency and God's endless supply?

When people see how you spend money, do they conclude that *God* is a priceless treasure, exceedingly valuable above all worldly goods?

When people observe your relationship with others, are they alerted to the power of Christ's forgiveness of you that alone accounts for your forgiveness of them?

When you open your mouth and speak of others in public (or private), are they made to think of Jesus in whose mouth no "deceit" was found (1 Pet. 2:22), the one who, when reviled, "did not revile in return" (1 Pet. 2:23)?

When you respond to injustice or mistreatment, are your words and ways the sort that lead them to glorify the God-man who "did not threaten" those who abused him "but continued entrusting himself to him who judges justly" (1 Pet. 2:23)?

When others see you interacting with people of another race, do they instinctively fix their thoughts on God's love for all without regard to color of skin or ethnic heritage?

If you are complimented for some accomplishment, does the way you receive it drive onlookers to give thanks to the Lord?

Do you preach the Word in such a way that eyes are riveted on you or turned upward to behold the beauty of Christ?

Is your use of leisure time or devotion to a hobby or how you speak of your wife the sort that persuades others that your heart is content with what God is for me in Christ?

Does your reaction to bad news produce in others doubt or fear, or does it inspire confidence to trust in God's providence?

When you feel disappointment or experience a shattered dream, is others' trust in God's promises diminished or enhanced?

Does your reaction to suffering inspire others to take comfort in him?

To use Paul's word, when you "minister" among others, are they captivated by your credentials or energized to find satisfaction in God's merciful sufficiency?

Paul couldn't have cared less about his own reputation, unless by seeing him others savored God. If his weakness magnified God's power, then by all means, watch. So long as his life was a window through which others might behold the goodness and grace of Christ, Paul was more than happy to commend himself to their scrutiny.

"Don't look *at* or *to* me," Paul said, "but *through* me, as a minister of God, to the fountain of all goodness and grace."

So again, when others see you, does *God* look good?

40

Examples of Endurance in Waco

2 Corinthians 6:4

But as servants of God we commend ourselves in every way: by great endurance, in afflictions, hardships, calamities.

In January 2008, my wife and I had the privilege of attending the World Mandate conference in Waco, Texas, sponsored by Antioch Community Church and Antioch Ministries International. This was our second time to make the trip south for what has proven on both occasions to be a marvelously instructive and encouraging experience.

World Mandate has one preeminent goal, regardless of the year or the speakers or the date when it is held. That goal is to awaken our hearts to the plight of a lost and dying world and to energize and equip both young and old to take the gospel of Christ's love to the nations of the earth.

Both years we attended we had the incredible privilege of hearing the testimonies of men and women who have happily turned their back on the comforts of Western society for the indescribable privilege (yes, *privilege*) of joyfully suffering for Christ's sake (yes, *joyfully*) so that his name and glory may be spread globally to those who have never heard the good news.

Ann and I have come away each time stunned by the courage and commitment of these people, inspired by their example, but most of all encouraged by their endurance. Endurance is an interesting word, both in English and in Greek. We often think of the marathon runner as displaying remarkable endurance by being able to run, without pause, for more than twenty-six miles. The word connotes the idea of a refusal to quit, a commitment to persevere in spite of the worst imaginable pain and the most oppressive of circumstances.

The Greek term translated "endurance" (*hupomone*) means much the same. It most often refers to the ability to stand up under pressure and to endure affliction without resorting to complaint or bitterness or a self-serving victim mentality.

Here in 2 Corinthians 6:4 it stands as something of a general heading or statement for what follows in the rest of the paragraph (vv. 4b–10). It is designed to indicate how the apostle Paul faithfully embraced the many expressions of adversity that he lists. In other words, how did Paul face up to "afflictions, hardships, and calamities" (v. 4b), or to "beatings, imprisonments, riots, labors, sleepless nights, and hunger" (v. 5)? He did it "by [or with] great endurance" (v. 4a).

I regret having to say this, but when I encounter trials of this sort (and I have yet to encounter them in the way that Paul did on a regular basis), it isn't with "great endurance" that I respond but with "great griping" or "much mumbling" or "constant complaining" or some such sinful attitude.

I didn't hear much, if any, of that at World Mandate. That isn't to say these folk are immune to the temptation to grow weak and weary. They struggle to persevere and often want to quit. But most of them don't. Something invisible sustains them. Their hearts are buoyed by an unseen power.

I think particularly of one friend that I met three years ago in Waco whose endurance in the face of adversity and repeated life-threatening incidents is such an encouragement to me and a reflection of what the apostle Paul himself describes here in 2 Corinthians 6:4–10. For his own protection (and that of his family), I won't mention his name or where he is planting a church, but it would be difficult to think of a more perilous place on earth. So how is he so determined, so relentless, so willing to put at risk his own welfare for the sake of lost souls? What accounts for this "great" and other-worldly "endurance"?

There are several ways to answer that question, but since it is Paul who makes the point in 2 Corinthians 6:4–10, I'll let his own words supply the reply. He writes:

> For whatever was written in former days was written for our instruc-tion, that *through endurance and through the encouragement of the Scriptures we might have hope.* May *the God of endurance* and encour-agement grant you to live in such harmony with one another, in accord with Christ Jesus. (Rom. 15:4–5)

Observe how God is described. He is "the God of endurance" (v. 5). That is to say, endurance finds its source in him. If we endure in a good and godly way, we must attribute it to him. It flows from his heart to ours.

All well and good, one might say. But *how* does he do it? Through what means or mechanism does God sustain weary souls and broken bodies and hearts threatened with disillusionment? Does endurance gently fall to earth like the manna of old, descending like dew for us to gather up and ingest? No, not exactly.

Paul couldn't have been clearer about how God imparts endur-ance and encouragement to the human heart: it is *through the Scrip-tures!* The "Scriptures" Paul has in view is, of course, the Old Testa-ment (for us today, it is the entire canon of inspired writ). This is God's ordained instrument for supplying us with the wherewithal to persevere, the ultimate purpose of which, he notes, is so that "we might have hope" (Rom. 15:4).

When the Word of God is read and heard and understood and believed, the Spirit uses it to produce steadfastness and strength to hold on in the face of what appears to be insurmountable opposi-tion. Paul is not talking about gritting our teeth against all odds. He has in mind hearts driven and sustained and upheld by "hope" that is itself the fruit of "endurance" that comes to us from the Scriptures.

So, how do the Scriptures impart "endurance"? How does God's Word encourage us and build and buoy hope in the hurting heart? Here's how.

When we meditate on the Scriptures, we see inspired portrayals of God's indescribable goodness that infinitely transcends anything the physical perks of Western society can supply.

When we study and muse on the Scriptures, we hear infallible promises of God's abiding presence no matter how lonely we may feel or how often others abandon us in time of need.

When we focus on the Scriptures, we are reminded of stories of God's faithfulness to others who have faced far worse than we have.

When we memorize the Scriptures, we are later reminded of God's inviolable purpose to bring us into glory through Jesus Christ no matter how resistant people may be or how determined they are to undermine our faith.

When we open our souls to the Scriptures, we are alerted to stirring accounts of God's power to defeat the most vile and vicious of enemies.

When we pray through the Scriptures, we are nourished by poetic descriptions of God's majesty and grandeur and love and kindness and splendor and glory.

And when we labor to understand the Scriptures, we learn of simple and oft-repeated truths about his compassion for his children, his forgiving of their sins, his covenant faithfulness, and his singing over them in passionate, heartfelt affection.

My friend in Waco isn't an extraordinarily strong man. He's not wealthy. He's smart, but not a genius. So why is he able to accomplish what others only dream of? Simply put, he exudes *great endurance*. He is upheld by persistent faith. His commitment is undying and unflagging. And all this from the God of endurance, imparted to him (and to us) through the Scriptures.

41

Feasting on the Promise of a Future with Christ

2 Corinthians 6:4–5

But as servants of God we commend ourselves in every way: by great endurance, in afflictions, hardships, calamities, beatings, imprisonments, riots, labors, sleepless nights, hunger.

There is hardly a time when I'm more keenly aware of my sinful and selfish orientation than when my personal comfort and convenience are threatened or interrupted. When I miss a meal, I'm grumpy. When the air conditioner breaks, I'm irritable. When I'm in pain, I complain. It grieves me to see how often I act as if I deserved physical security and emotional peace and a full stomach. I'm stunned by how much time, energy, and money I devote to avoid what makes for turmoil and discomfort.

Now, I'm not at all suggesting that a person should actively seek those things that breed distress or anguish or deprivation. People who do are either masochistic or suffer from a perverted martyr complex. There's nothing inherently good in pain. In fact, it is part of our calling as Christians to help alleviate the suffering and hardship of others. But in doing so, it may well require that we ourselves willingly embrace danger or the loss of freedom and property, as well as the disruption of our cherished routines and schedules.

No one knew this better than Paul, a man who personally suffered almost indescribable agony for the sake of Christ and the welfare of his people. It's hard for me to read Paul's description of his life and not see in it a standing rebuke and counterargument to the health and wealth "gospel" of the twenty-first century. Today, sadly, we are often told that if you are among God's "anointed" and "gifted" and "favored" servants you can expect (even claim) exemption from suffering, loss, and deprivation. You're a "child of the King" and thus deserve "first-class" treatment. This was similar to the argument of Paul's opponents in Corinth, who insisted that a true "apostle" of Christ would never endure the things he did. It was precisely this alleged lack of so-called *apostolic credentials* that people used to undermine his authority and authenticity in that church.

Evidently people asked Paul on numerous occasions to substantiate his claim to apostolic authority. Although he detested speaking of himself, the situation at Corinth required that he identify his qualifications. He does so on several occasions (see esp. 11:16–33), one of the more explicit being here in 6:4–10. "Do you want me to commend myself for your approval?" he asked. "So be it. I'm happy to present myself to you as a minister of God, and on the following grounds":

> by great endurance, in afflictions, hardships, calamities, beatings, imprisonments, riots, labors, sleepless nights, hunger; by purity, knowledge, patience, kindness, the Holy Spirit, genuine love; by truthful speech, and the power of God; with the weapons of righteousness for the right hand and for the left; through honor and dishonor, through slander and praise. We are treated as impostors, and yet are true; as unknown, and yet well known; as dying, and behold, we live; as punished, and yet not killed; as sorrowful, yet always rejoicing; as poor, yet making many rich; as having nothing, yet possessing everything. (2 Cor. 6:4–10)

Our focus in this meditation is on verses 4–5 in which we find three sets of three words that describe Paul's outward circumstances, all of which, it should be noted, are in the plural, indicating multiple instances or occasions on which he suffered.

In the first set of three he mentions "afflictions, hardships, calamities." "Afflictions" is a general and all-encompassing term appearing numerous times in 2 Corinthians, the most severe of which was the life-threatening experience Paul described in 1:8–9. "Hardships" carries the thought of being under pressure, perhaps an allusion to the constant stress to which he was subjected. The word translated "calamities" literally means "in constraints" or in a confined and narrow place from which there can be no escape. It points to Paul's feeling of being trapped by circumstances seemingly beyond his control.

The second set of three points more to the direct and extremely physical persecution to which he was subjected. He often endured "beatings" (see 11:23–25), whether by rods, lashes, or fists. We know specifically of only one "imprisonment" (see 2 Cor. 11:23) before 2 Corinthians was written, which occurred in Philippi (Acts 16). This indicates that Luke's history in Acts is obviously selective and does not purport to give us an exhaustive record of Paul's missionary experiences.

The "riots" or uprisings against Paul in the cities where he preached are numerous: at Pisidian Antioch (Acts 13:50), Iconium (Acts 14:5), Lystra (Acts 14:19), Philippi (Acts 16:22), Thessalonica (Acts 17:5–7), Berea (Acts 17:13), Corinth (Acts 18:12–17), and Ephesus (Acts 19:23–20:1).

Finally, he endured "labors, sleepless nights, [and] hunger." Unlike the first six words that describe what was done to him by others, these all refer to *self-imposed* hardships Paul embraced in the fulfillment of his ministry.

The word "labors" is either a reference to his work as a tentmaker (Acts 18:3) or to his extended and demanding seasons of work as a missionary, pastor, and evangelist.

By "sleeplessness" he doesn't mean that he suffered from insomnia, but that he voluntarily went without sleep to serve and minister to others (Paul often refers to working "night and day"; see 1 Thess. 2:9; 2 Thess. 3:8). Whether he lost sleep from working late hours to support himself or because he was engaged in ministry late into the night, it was a choice he joyfully embraced.

Finally, he often suffered from "hunger." There's little agreement on any single cause for this. It certainly could be a reference to his frequent fasting. Others see a self-imposed asceticism designed to alleviate any burden from those to whom he ministered. Or it could simply be a reference to his lack of food due to the hardships of travel or even the lack of money.

I travel extensively throughout the United States and occasionally overseas, speaking at churches and conferences. Typically, either at some point while I'm away or immediately upon my return, my wife lovingly asks such questions as: "Did the ministry go well? Did they respond positively to what you had to say? Did you sleep well in the hotel? At what restaurants did you eat? Are you feeling OK?"

She's never yet heard me say in reply: "They threw stones at me during my first sermon. One caught me square in the forehead. I felt my life was in jeopardy on a few occasions, and I honestly didn't know if I'd escape. Two leaders in the church beat me with rods and the local sheriff threw me in jail on the second night. I didn't sleep a wink in that stinking cell, and the food was so repulsive I couldn't eat a thing. Other than that, the ministry was great!"

No one in the Christian West anticipates such treatment. If we ever encountered anything remotely similar to what Paul faced, we'd wipe the dust from our shoes and never return. Surely "servants of God" (v. 4) who are dedicated to the gospel ought to expect the best of everything. How dare anyone deprive us of our comforts!

So what would motivate a man to willingly pursue a life characterized by the sort of hardships Paul endured? What could possibly sustain a man through such sufferings?

One answer is found in Hebrews 10:32–34. There we read of Christians who "endured a hard struggle with sufferings, sometimes being publicly exposed to reproach and affliction, and sometimes being partners with those so treated" (vv. 32–33). Beyond this, they "joyfully accepted the plundering" of their "property" (v. 34)! Here's why. Here's how. They "knew" they "had a better possession and an abiding one" (v. 34).

The degree to which we find suffering intolerable is the degree to which we lack confidence in the glory of our inheritance in Christ.

To the extent that we are embittered by oppression and persecution, we reveal our lack of satisfaction in him.

Paul was in the grip of the glory to come (see 2 Cor. 4:16–18) and found strength to endure. Like those believers in Hebrews 10, he feasted on the promise of a future with Christ and held fast.

42

What's a Christian to Do?

2 Corinthians 6:6–7

By purity, knowledge, patience, kindness, the Holy Spirit, genuine
love; by truthful speech, and the power of God; with the weapons
of righteousness for the right hand and for the left.

W hat's a Christian to do? In a world of increasing contempt for the gospel and, more often than not, overt
and unapologetic opposition, how is a follower of Jesus
to respond? In the face of legislation that undermines our moral
convictions, a secular atheism that marginalizes our presence, and a
radical Islamic fundamentalism that seeks our utter eradication, is
the Christian a helpless pawn in the chess game of global maneuver-
ing? Do we fight back, and if so, how? With what weapons? With
what expectations?

It would be easy for the church to feel overwhelmed and under-
manned. Abortion is law. Disdain for our cherished beliefs is com-
monplace. Moral decay is embraced as progress.

Just recently I read of a parachurch ministry that was banned
from a university campus for its opposition to homosexuality, a
professor who was denied tenure because of his research on intel-

ligent design, and a group of Christians who were denied a zoning permit to plant a church in a residential neighborhood. And all the while Satan seems to be gaining ground. So, what's a Christian to do?

The opposition may have assumed a different form in the first century, when Paul was asking the same question, but the response of the Christian is the same in any and every age. When assaulted, afflicted, beaten or imprisoned, when pressured, persecuted, weakened or weary, here's how we fight: "by purity, [by] knowledge, [by] patience, [by] kindness, [by] the Holy Spirit, [by] genuine love; by truthful speech, and the power of God; with the weapons of righteousness for the right hand and for the left" (2 Cor. 6:6–7).

"Oh, come on, Sam. Get real. We're talking about a battle of monumental proportions. Our enemies are clever and well-equipped. They will stop at nothing to destroy the body of Christ. They are relentless and ruthless. They will use any tactic, legal or not, to win. They have unlimited financial resources, unchecked political power, and numbers that dwarf us. And here you are recommending that we fight back with pious, pie-in-the-sky-by-and-by spiritual platitudes! Give me a break! Do you really believe that the things Paul mentions here are of any value in a war that threatens to consume and destroy us?"

Well, yes.

I'm not suggesting that we withdraw from the political process or roll over and play dead. God has graciously given us laws and a variety of secular institutions and opportunities that enhance our lives and provide for the protection of the church. But our ultimate confidence and trust must be in something greater still.

In the list of nine, we begin with "purity" of motivation and behavior. Paul has already referred to his renunciation of dishonesty and his refusal to stoop to underhanded and crafty tactics (see 2 Cor. 4:2). Simple purity has a power to effect change and to commend the gospel far beyond any political shenanigans.

The "knowledge" or "understanding" in view probably refers not simply to theological insight but to the practical discernment in Paul as he dealt with his enemies in Corinth.

Instead of retaliation and revenge, "patience" is the order of the day when facing the indignities and insults of others. Whereas "endurance" (v. 4) is courage and perseverance while suffering unjustified adversity, "patience" or "longsuffering" is "the forbearance which endures injuries and evil deeds without being provoked to anger (James 1:19) or vengeance (Rom. 12:19)."[1]

Simple "kindness" accomplishes far more than we can imagine. Ann and I were recently in the townhome of a dear friend whose new neighbor had embarked on a drunken, obscene, and violent tirade. Well past midnight, he banged on the walls and shouted vile threats. The next day, our friend took a plate of cookies next door, declaring her intentions to be a good neighbor and available to help if ever there were a need. The sinful rage of the night before has yet to reappear.

The reference to the "Holy Spirit" strikes some as odd, appearing as it does in the middle of a list of Christian virtues. Some say it is the human spirit in view, but every other time Paul uses the adjective "holy" with the noun "spirit" it refers to the Holy Spirit. Perhaps the difficulty is minimized if we understand Paul to be referring to the gifts of the Holy Spirit. Or perhaps he included this reference to the Spirit upon realizing that the purity, understanding, patience, and kindness he mentioned are themselves the fruit of the Spirit (see Gal. 5:22–23).

The phrase "in genuine love" calls for some explanation. The Greek term *hupocrites*, from which we derive our word "hypocrite," was used in reference to a person who played a part on the stage, an actor, someone who took on a role different from what he was in reality. Thus when this word is negated (*anupokrito*), as it is here in 2 Corinthians 6:6, it carries the force of "not good at acting on a stage" and thus "free from pretense" or "without hypocrisy" and thus *sincere* or *genuine*. Love that is feigned or that masks selfish desires only destroys. Love that is authentic commends the gospel and changes others.

In light of Paul's earlier reference to "the open statement of the truth" (2 Cor. 4:2) as something that characterizes his ministry, the phrase "by truthful speech" (lit., "by the word of truth") here in verse 6 most likely has in view his declaring of the truth of the gospel. Certainly his relationships with others were characterized by truthfulness and honesty, but his focus here is on the power of the preached and proclaimed truth of a dying and rising Savior.

Needless to say, "the power of God" alone explains how all of the preceding and following are even possible. Without the energizing presence of God, nothing we say or do will have effect.

Yes, we are in a battle. No, our weapons are not physical, mechanical, political, or computerized. Rather, we fight "with the weapons of righteousness for the right hand and for the left" (v. 7). A soldier in Paul's day would typically wield a sword in his right hand, designed for attack, and a shield in the left for defense. As such, he was fully prepared to rebuff an assault from any direction.

Life-changing, world-winning power is not ultimately found in the speed of a computer chip or the most sophisticated satellite technology, far less in the military strategies of global superpowers. True power, the power that brings life to dead souls and hope to despairing hearts, the sort of power that renews and uplifts and sustains, the power that commends and adorns the gospel, is found in the simple but supernatural weapons of a pure heart, a clear head, forbearance, kindness, the manifestation of the Spirit, a love untouched by hypocrisy, truthfulness in speech, and the power of God energizing the weapons of our warfare for the sake of his kingdom.

It may not be "cool" or "sexy" or the sort of life that captures the attention of the media or powerbrokers in our world, but it's what God has given us. It worked for Paul, and I trust it will work for us.

43

The Treasure, Quite Simply, Is Christ

2 Corinthians 6:8–9

Through honor and dishonor, through slander and praise. We are treated as impostors, and yet are true; as unknown, and yet well known; as dying, and behold, we live; as punished, and yet not killed.

On June 22, 1750, Jonathan Edwards was fired. After twenty-four years of ministry at the church in Northampton, Massachusetts, twenty-one of which he served as senior pastor, America's greatest pastor-theologian was dismissed by an overwhelming vote of the male membership (women were not allowed to vote).

Edwards's response? After enduring years of theological wrangling, bitter opposition, rancorous slander, and malicious gossip, one might have expected him either to wallow in self-pity or lash out in angry recriminations. Not Edwards. One observer described his reaction in these memorable words:

That faithful witness received the shock, unshaken. I never saw the least symptoms of displeasure in his countenance the whole week, but he appeared like a man of God, whose happiness was out of the reach of his enemies and whose treasure was not only a future but a present good, overbalancing all imaginable ills of life, even to the astonishment of many who could not be at rest without his dismission [i.e., dismissal].[1]

Edwards was a pastor, not an apostle, but he had obviously learned much from Paul's experience. Something was at work in both men that elevated their happiness beyond the grasp of even the most vicious of their enemies. A treasure of inestimable value more than compensated for "all imaginable ills of life."

Nowhere does Paul say it with greater clarity than here in 2 Corinthians 6, as he describes a ministry and a life characterized by great endurance in the midst of afflictions, hardships, calamities, beatings, imprisonments, riots, labors, sleepless nights, and hunger (vv. 4–5). He responded to such trials with purity, knowledge, patience, kindness, love, and truth, all in the power of God through the Holy Spirit (vv. 6–7).

The paradox of Paul's experience is nothing short of stunning. I want to briefly note the first six of these paradoxical pairs in verses 8–9.

We love it when others hold us in high regard ("honor," v. 8). A good reputation is easy to live with. But "dishonor" is something else. When people hold opinions of us shaped by misinformation and unjustified criticism, we either respond in kind or retreat to a defensive posture. All too often our emotional equilibrium fluctuates with our public opinion poll. We're high when the numbers are. When the polls go down, so do we.

Paul was neither overinflated by "praise" nor destroyed by "slander" (v. 8). He could enjoy public affirmation without becoming dependent upon it. He was largely unaffected by what others thought of him. This is stunning when one considers the customary defamation he endured at Corinth. Notwithstanding his most humble and self-sacrificial posture, he was often excoriated and denounced. The Corinthians accused him of being fickle (2 Cor. 1:17), of being motivated by worldly ambition (10:2), and for falling short in regard to physical appearance and lacking verbal eloquence.

"We are treated as impostors, and yet are true" (v. 8). Paul is in good company here, as Jesus himself was regarded as a deceiver by his enemies (see John 7:12; Matt. 27:63). Yet we know that Paul's calling was genuine (Gal. 1:1, 15–16), his message was authentic (2 Cor. 4:2; 6:7), and he consistently spoke the truth (2 Cor. 11:31; Rom. 9:1; Gal. 1:20; 1 Tim. 2:7).

What does he mean in saying he was "unknown, and yet well known" (v. 9)? Some say this refers to views of Paul held outside the church (he's an unknown quantity, insignificant, uncelebrated, easily ignored) versus inside the church (respected and acknowledged). More likely a human perspective is being contrasted with a divine one. The false teachers in Corinth, together with some of the members there, refused to recognize him as an apostle. But God did (see 2 Cor. 1:1). And it's the latter's opinion that mattered to Paul.

There may even be a more personal dimension to this contrast. Yes, he was largely unknown to the world, a "nobody," if you will. Yet God knew him, loved him, and cherished him as a good and faithful son. "The Lord knows those who are his" (2 Tim. 2:19; cf. John 10:14), Paul wrote to young Timothy. And the apostle was no exception. Others may forget who I am, Paul says, but the Lord Jesus has written down my name in the Lamb's book of life (see Luke 10:20; Phil. 4:3)!

Yes, we are constantly exposed to life-threatening circumstances ("as dying," v. 9), yet "we live" (see 2 Cor. 1:8–9; 4:11–18; 1 Cor. 15:30–31; Acts 14:19–20). We are "punished" but "not killed" (v. 9), knowing that "all discipline seems painful rather than pleasant, but later it yields the peaceful fruit of righteousness to those who have been trained by it" (Heb. 12:11).

What has to happen in the human heart to make such a life possible? How does one attain to this perspective? Is there a formula? A magical incantation? A prayer to pray? A task to perform? What accounts for the presence of joy rather than bitterness in Paul's soul? How was he able to keep his happiness "out of the reach of his enemies"?

For this, we must return to the words of that astute observer in 1750. His "treasure," this man wrote of Edwards, "was not only a future but a present good, overbalancing all imaginable ills of life."

Something was of such immeasurable value that Edwards happily let go of all earthly goods and gain. There was something he prized above the praise of men. The root of his dependency on the accolades of others was severed by his delight in a far surpassing pleasure.

Edwards (like Paul) was captivated by a treasure so radiant that he was blinded to the light of fool's gold. Its glorious sound rendered him deaf to the slander of his enemies. The sweetness of this "present good" turned sin sour in his soul. He had experienced a joy so satisfying and a pleasure so all-consuming that "all imaginable ills of life" dwindled in their capacity to embitter or enslave. The treasure, quite simply, was Christ.

44

Spiritual Schizophrenia

2 Corinthians 6:10

As sorrowful, yet always rejoicing; as poor, yet making many rich; as having nothing, yet possessing everything.

One definition of "schizophrenia" is "a situation or condition that results from the coexistence of disparate or antagonistic qualities, identities, or activities."[1] Another entry reads: "a state characterized by the coexistence of contradictory or incompatible elements."

Given these definitions, there is a sense in which Christianity gives every appearance of being schizophrenic! There are in the Christian life, and in that of the apostle Paul in particular, situations or conditions or states of mind, if you will, that strike those outside the believing community (and more than a few on the inside as well) as being disparate or antagonistic or contradictory or incompatible.

If that sounds outlandish to you, meditate for a few moments on Paul's description of his life and ministry as portrayed here in 2 Corinthians 6:10. I am, Paul said, "sorrowful, yet always rejoicing." Although I am "poor" I make "many rich." I have "nothing," he confessed, yet I possess "everything"!

I want to say, "Make up your mind, Paul! You can't have it both ways. Sorrow and joy are incompatible. Poverty and riches are disparate, mutually exclusive states of being." No wonder non-Christians think we're crazy.

What accounts for Paul's admittedly odd perspective on life? Is he emotionally unstable, a dreamer, a man who's lost touch with reality, or someone who has a deep and profound grasp on what is of ultimate value? I suggest it is the latter.

Let's be clear about one thing. If there is no life beyond the grave, Paul is certifiably insane. If this world is all there has been, is, or ever will be, it is senseless to speak of joy in the midst of suffering or to regard oneself as wealthy in the face of poverty. The value system that accounts for Paul's point of view is one shaped by a belief in the reality of eternity, a life everlasting in which never-ending good prevails over evil, an existence in which the beauty and splendor of Jesus Christ provide ceaseless and ever-increasing satisfaction that transcends anything this current life can afford.

Paul's "sorrow" was very real. His anticipation of eternal joy did not negate the hardships of life, but it did make them bearable. We misunderstand the apostle, and Christianity as a whole, if we believe the Bible is telling us to ignore pain or pretend that it is less agonizing than it is.

The source of his sorrow was multifaceted. He felt "great sorrow and unceasing anguish" (Rom. 9:2) over the lost estate of his Jewish brethren. His often tumultuous relationship with the Corinthians was the source of "much affliction and anguish of heart" (2 Cor. 2:4). Then there was "the daily pressure" of his "anxiety for all the churches" (2 Cor. 11:28), not to mention the sadness he felt upon seeing Christ scorned and mocked, as well as his own sufferings from persecution and slander.

Yet, we are told, he was "always rejoicing"! This can only be explained in light of two factors. First, he must have believed that even the worst of circumstances and the most oppressive of trials were subject to an overriding and gracious providence. Were it not for his belief that "all things work together for good" for those who love God and are called according to his purpose (Rom. 8:28), he could not have rejoiced simultaneously with his sorrow. It was not wishful thinking but *the most rigorous spiritual realism* that enabled him to endure, knowing that whatever befell him was sovereignly designed to facilitate his conformity "to the image" of God's Son, Jesus Christ (Rom. 8:29).

Second, there must have been a deep and abiding well of spiritual refreshment from which he regularly drew that provided his heart with incomparable and life-sustaining satisfaction, something so fascinating, enthralling, and captivating that no root of bitterness could thrive or disillusionment could displace. As we've seen repeatedly, this well was the goodness and grace of the Lord Jesus Christ himself (see 2 Cor. 12:9–10).

Even when joy in the present felt incomplete and distant and strained, Paul labored to savor the foretaste of future delight in God, no doubt constantly reminding himself that "the sufferings of this present time are not worth comparing with the glory that is to be revealed to us" (Rom. 8:18). Clearly, true joy is not dependent on pleasant circumstances. It is possible to rejoice in a way that is genuine and real and sincere and unfeigned while yet enduring trials that in themselves have the potential to bring only misery and despair.

The apparent spiritual schizophrenia continues when Paul describes himself "as poor, yet making many rich." What could he possibly mean by this? Obviously both can't be literal, for Paul would never have thought of himself as increasing the financial wealth of the churches where he ministered. That would simply have never factored into the goals he set for his work among the congregations he founded.

Paul probably meant it literally in saying that he was "poor." In his first letter to the Corinthians he wrote: "To the present hour we hunger and thirst, we are poorly dressed and buffeted and homeless, and we labor, working with our own hands . . ." (1 Cor. 4:11–12; an important reminder for all aspiring apostles!). Paul's work as a tentmaker provided him with only basic necessities. But his poverty was a matter of choice. He wanted to avoid any possibility that people might think he was in the ministry for the money (2 Cor. 11:7–12; 1 Cor. 9:12, 15, 18), and he never wanted to be a burden to his converts (see 2 Cor. 11:9; 12:13, 16).

Yet, he was not in the least bothered by his material deprivation, for it served to enhance the opportunity "to enrich" others spiritually and for eternity. Paul uses this verb in 1 Corinthians 1:5 where he describes the believers in that church as "in every way" "enriched in him [i.e., in Christ] in all speech and all knowledge" (see 2 Cor. 9:11).

Although Paul himself lacked earthly riches, he delighted in imparting to others "the unsearchable riches of Christ" (Eph. 3:8) and the "surpassing worth of knowing" Christ Jesus as Lord (Phil. 3:8; cf. Rom. 10:12; 11:12). He labored among the Colossians to make known "the riches of the glory of this mystery, which is Christ in you, the hope of glory" (Col. 1:27).

Nothing could be more obvious than this: if Christ is not himself a treasure of incomparable worth, a prize of incalculable value, a source of ineffable satisfaction, material hardship will only serve to embitter and harden your heart.

Finally, though I have nothing, Paul said, I possess everything! But he surely had a few worldly possessions, and would never have claimed ownership in sin and ill-gotten gain. This is undoubtedly rhetorical hyperbole, designed to highlight the infinitely superior blessings of Christ and the age to come. Although he owned little in terms of transient and worldly goods, Paul considered himself opulent when it came to things eternal and of infinite spiritual value.

"So let no one boast in men," he wrote to the Corinthians. "For *all things are yours*, whether Paul or Apollos or Cephas or the world or life or death or the present or the future—all are yours, and you are Christ's, and Christ is God's" (1 Cor. 3:21–23).

If we are able to embrace a thoroughly biblical worldview, a perspective in which the values of eternity impinge on the present, we will always appear schizophrenic to those who do not know Christ as Lord and Savior.

Without him, sorrow trumps joy, and material gain becomes our only reasonable goal. With him, joy flourishes in the midst of all, even financial lack or physical pain.

45

Dealing with Dysfunction in the Family of Faith

2 Corinthians 6:11–13

We have spoken freely to you, Corinthians; our heart is wide open. You are not restricted by us, but you are restricted in your own affections. In return (I speak as to children) widen your hearts also.

I recently received an e-mail from a reader who was lamenting the tragic absence of love in the body of Christ. He was grieved by the failure of many to take seriously the words of John, who insisted that "whoever loves God *must* also love his brother" (1 John 4:21).

The failure of the church to love its own is an ugly blemish on the public face of Christianity. All of us have seen it, and many have felt its pain. There are countless reasons why this is a such a problem: fear, lack of trust, suspicion, past failures, grudges, unforgiveness, anger, and broken promises, most of which is fueled by pride, ambition, insecurity, greed, gossip and, well, perhaps you should just finish the list.

One of the many strengths of Scripture is its refusal to sugarcoat the relational dysfunction among its more prominent characters. I suppose some might have preferred that Paul not publicize his

215

struggles with the Corinthians. They wonder why the Spirit preserved for us so many ugly episodes. I, for one, am glad he did. How else are we to learn principles for conflict resolution? How else can we grow in relational harmony and overcome the many obstacles that hinder our witness to a lost and dying world?

That there was a palpable tension between them is evident from Paul's words in 2 Corinthians 6:11–13. Although brief, close examination of this paragraph will yield great wisdom for resolving our interpersonal struggles in the body of Christ.

Most of us have, at one time or another, been on both sides of this sort of dispute. Like the Corinthians, you may have developed a lack of trust for leadership in the church. Fueled by gossip and misinformation, you may have grown to doubt their sincerity or their honesty. Perhaps you view them as power hungry and insensitive to the needs of others. One of your friends or family members may have been hurt by excessive authority or unjustly removed from a place of ministry. As a result, there is little room left for them in your heart.

On the other hand, you, like Paul, may have been the object of unwarranted criticism. Notwithstanding your best efforts and most sacrificial labors, people misinterpret your motives and impugn your character. You may wonder, *After all I've done and everything I've given, you'd think they'd give me the benefit of the doubt.*

Regardless of which side of the fence you're on, it hurts. You expect Christians to live by a higher standard. You're shocked when their behavior differs little from what you encounter in the world at large. When your best efforts to put things right come up short, it seems only reasonable to withdraw, shut down your heart, elevate your guard, and wait for them to make the first move.

It's clear from Paul's words in this passage that he didn't embrace that philosophy. His approach to resolution is refreshing and highly instructive. We would do well to imitate his strategy. I'd like to highlight five principles at work in Paul's relationship with the Corinthians from which we can learn much.

The first thing that stands out to me is the deeply personal and direct way in which Paul addresses them. Did you notice his use of the word "Corinthians" (not simply "you"), as well as his appeal to them as his "children" (only elsewhere in Gal. 3:1 and Phil. 4:15 does he address his readers by name)?

The reference to them as "children" is not a rebuke, as if Paul is saying that they are acting "childishly." Rather, these believers are his children "in the faith" (see 1 Tim. 1:2). Paul led them to Christ. He was the human instrument in their spiritual birth. This is an affirmation of intimacy, not indignation.

It's not easy to speak in such terms to those who've hurt you badly. Your instinct is to keep them at arm's length and not to expose yourself until you're convinced of their good intentions. But Paul won't have it. He is open and up front about his feelings for them. This is not a guarded or dispassionate command on his part but a heartfelt appeal from a spiritual father to his spiritual children.

A second principle to note is the transparent and honest way in which Paul lets his heart be known. He holds back nothing. He hides no motives, employs no facades, and avoids all pretense. He turns away from verbal manipulation and speaks the truth without embellishment or flair.

The fact that Paul's frank speech is an accurate and utterly honest expression of his intentions and beliefs and desires is indicated by the second phrase, "our heart is wide open." Jesus declared that "out of the abundance of the heart the mouth speaks" (Matt. 12:34), and Paul hopes the Corinthians will hear his words and thereby feel the pulse of his soul. He knows they are still suspicious of him. He knows they harbor ill will. He knows they doubt his sincerity. He knows they are afraid of entrusting themselves to him. Yet this is no hindrance to his complete openness.

The phrase, "we have spoken freely to you," is literally "our mouth is open toward you," a graphic and pointed way of describing utterly unrestrained, vulnerable, frank speech. Paul here is uninhibited and free in expressing his affections.

Third, be prepared to correct false notions or unwarranted beliefs that others have about your feelings. Paul knew they thought he loved them little (see 2 Cor. 11:11). So here he uses a figure of speech called *litotes*, in which a positive is emphasized by use of the negative. Thus when he says "you are not restricted by us" he means, in effect, "you enjoy the fullest devotion possible," or "we love you with unbridled affection," or more literally, "I have not allowed you to be squeezed out of my heart."

Fourth, identify the problem. Don't skirt around the issue or pretend that it is less painful than it is. Be specific in focusing on the source of the tension. You may be wrong, but at least it will let others know how you perceive the situation. In this case, Paul is convinced that the problem is not that he lacks affection for them, but that they have shut their hearts toward him. "You are restricted in your own affections," he says. The word translated "affections" is a graphic one in Greek (*splanchna*), referring to the inward parts, the viscera or entrails, if you will. It is obviously a metaphor for the emotions or feelings or deep affections.

Paul unashamedly declares that they have failed to reciprocate his love. His feelings for them are honest and sincere and passionate. He has not closed himself to their needs or their pain. But they in turn have not returned the favor. If he is open, they are closed.

Fifth, Paul makes an urgent and heartfelt appeal to them. In return for opening his heart to them, he pleads that they will open theirs to him. "In medical terms," notes Murray Harris, "an enlarged heart is a dangerous liability; in spiritual terms, an enlarged heart is a productive asset."[1]

Paul doesn't bludgeon them with heavy-handed ecclesiastical power, but speaks to them as a friend and a father. He doesn't play the apostolic trump card to enforce his will, but entreats and pleads with tender passion. His spirit isn't official, but personal.

Does it always work? Sadly, no. There will always be people in the church who, in a perverse sort of way, derive pleasure and sinful satisfaction from the alienation they have both caused and continue to perpetuate. Often their identity is wrapped up in the offense they carry. For others, to release it and reconcile requires a vulnerability they are not yet willing to embrace.

But their weakness is no excuse for our reluctance. Paul, it seems clear to me, was determined to obey his own command, painful though it be: "Repay no one evil for evil," he wrote to the Roman church, "but give thought to do what is honorable in the sight of all. If possible, so far as it depends on you, live peaceably with all" (Rom. 12:17–18). That's not easy to do, but the alternative is simply not an option for the one who says he "loves God" (1 John 4:21).

46

The Life of the Church in the World versus the Life of the World in the Church

2 Corinthians 6:14–16

Do not be unequally yoked with unbelievers. For what partnership has righteousness with lawlessness? Or what fellowship has light with darkness? What accord has Christ with Belial? Or what portion does a believer share with an unbeliever? What agreement has the temple of God with idols? . . .

What does it mean to be *in* the world but not *of* it? How is a Christian supposed to relate to those who despise and ridicule the name of Christ? To what extent are we to engage with the surrounding culture? Should a Christian shop at a store owned by a cult? Is the boycott an essential and effective expression of the church's protest against immorality in our society?

These are tough questions for which quick and overly-confident answers are unwise, and usually wrong. Although the culture has changed and the circumstances often differ greatly, the approach

Paul advocates in the first century still has relevance and binding moral authority for us today.

"Do not be unequally yoked with unbelievers . . ." (2 Cor. 6:14). One hears people quote this passage almost as often as John 3:16, but with considerably less clarity and understanding. What does Paul have in mind? What is the background to his exhortation, and how does it apply to us in the twenty-first century?

The situation in view was not a new one for Paul, having addressed it earlier in 1 Corinthians 6:12–20 and 8:1–11:1. Some professing Christians in Corinth were visiting the temple cults of any number of the pagan religions in the city, perhaps even engaging in the sexual activities (such as temple prostitution) associated with their "worship."

This problem was most likely the reason for Paul's emergency second visit to Corinth and the follow-up "severe letter" (see 2 Cor. 2:1–4; 10:1–6; 12:20–13:2). Therefore, the "unbelievers" that he describes in this passage were unconverted Gentiles who were involved in worship at the Greco-Roman mystery cults of Corinth (see the use of the word in 2 Cor. 4:4). His command, then, would be for Christian men and women to withdraw from such unholy and immoral alliances. But does the *principle* behind the imperative extend to other issues that we face today? Yes, but we must proceed cautiously in our application.

Although Paul is not thinking about marriage in this text, certainly the principle would prohibit a Christian entering into such a covenant with a non-Christian (1 Cor. 7:12–15, 39). Just as we are commanded not to put asunder what God has joined together, we must be diligent not to join together what God has put asunder!

Sadly, though, some have applied this passage in ways that Paul never sanctioned and that would, in effect, make it difficult even to live, much less work, in a secular society.

For example, there's no indication that Paul is forbidding or condemning all contact and association with non-Christians (something he declares impractical, if not impossible, in 1 Cor. 5:9–13). Indeed, he anticipates the presence of unbelievers in the worship services at Corinth and instructs the Corinthian believers not to do anything that might drive them away (1 Cor. 14:22–24).

Neither is he forbidding or condemning business relations with non-Christians. Whereas I believe it is biblically permissible (necessary?) to do business with a non-Christian, entering into a legal partnership with one calls for discernment and caution.

Paul is in no way forbidding or condemning friendships with non-Christians. If anything, I believe he would encourage them. But even then, *how close is too close* when it comes to fellowship with the unregenerate?

There is certainly nothing here that would forbid or condemn association and cooperation with other Christians who may disagree with you on secondary issues (contra the attitude in much of early Fundamentalism in Western religious culture). And contrary to what some have suggested, if two unbelievers marry and one subsequently comes to faith, Paul is not instructing the latter to terminate the relationship (see 1 Cor. 7:12–15).

As far as contemporary application is concerned, the *separation* Paul has in mind between Christians and non-Christians is *spiritual* and *moral*, not *spatial*. The principle is this: enter into no relationship or bond or partnership or endeavor that will compromise your Christian integrity or weaken your will for holiness or cast a shadow on your reputation (see James 4:4–5).

Some of the questions we must ask ourselves, in the effort to apply this principle, include:

"When I am with these nonbelievers, do I find myself in situations where I am unduly and dangerously exposed to temptation that may get the better of me?"

"When I am with non-Christians, do I find it easier than at other times to compromise on ethical matters? Do I find myself judging as "grey" what I would call "black" if I were with Christians?"

"Does my association with non-Christians tend to make me less vocal about my faith or less visible in my stand for Christ?"

"When I am with non-Christians, does conversation focus primarily on things of the world, or is there also opportunity for discussion of spiritual matters?"

"Does my association with non-Christians serve as an offense to others or a cause of reproach to the gospel?"

There then follow in 6:14–16 five pointed, rhetorical questions, each of which calls for the answer: "None whatsoever!"

> For what partnership has righteousness with lawlessness? Or what fellowship has light with darkness? What accord has Christ with Belial? Or what portion does a believer share with an unbeliever? What agreement has the temple of God with idols? . . . (2 Cor. 6:14–16)

These are designed to explain why it's important for believers to be cautious about having too close of an association with nonbelievers. Those committed to righteousness have no partnership with people given to lawlessness. Those who live in the light of God's revelation are not to be yoked with those who walk in spiritual and moral darkness. Quite obviously, Christ and the devil agree on nothing and have no harmony with one another. This is the only place in the New Testament where the word "Belial" occurs. Its Hebrew counterpart occurs in the Old Testament with the meaning "worthlessness" (e.g., Deut. 13:13; 15:9; 2 Sam. 22:5; Ps. 18:4), while in the intertestamental literature it was used to describe a personal opponent of God.

Likewise, a believer and nonbeliever share no *spiritual* common ground. As Philip Hughes has said,

> The unbeliever's life is centered on self, the believer's on Christ; the treasure of the one is here on earth, of the other in heaven; the values of the one are those of this world, of the other those of the world to come; the believer seeks the glory of God, the unbeliever the glory of men.[1]

However, Paul is not denying our common humanity or suggesting that there is literally nothing that we share. As John Calvin wisely reminds us, "when Paul says that the Christian has no portion with the unbeliever he is not referring to food, clothing, estates, the sun, and the air, . . . but to those things which are peculiar to unbelievers, from which the Lord has separated us."[2]

Finally, if the Old Testament prohibited the introduction of idols into the temple of God, how much more horrendous is idolatry in the life of the believer (v. 16)! Are we not ourselves the only temple in which God shall ever dwell (see 1 Cor. 3:16–17; 6:19; 2 Cor. 6:16b; Eph. 2:20–22; 1 Pet. 2:5)? Yes!

The significance of the believer as the temple of God will be taken up in the next meditation. Here I only wish to emphasize again the importance of discernment when it comes to forging relationships and partnerships with the unsaved.

What is most important to remember, then, is that this is "not a call to create a Christian ghetto, but a summons to purify the Christian community. *Paul does not have in view the life of the church in the world, but the life of the world in the church.*"[3] The former is both good and inevitable. The latter must be avoided at all costs.

We Are the Temple of the Living God

2 Corinthians 6:16–7:1

For we are the temple of the living God; as God said,

"I will make my dwelling among them and walk among them,
    and I will be their God,
    and they shall be my people.
Therefore go out from their midst,
    and be separate from them, says the Lord,
and touch no unclean thing;
    then I will welcome you,
and I will be a father to you,
    and you shall be sons and daughters to me,
says the Lord Almighty."

Since we have these promises, beloved, let us cleanse ourselves from every defilement of body and spirit, bringing holiness to completion in the fear of God.

On the one hand, I don't want to be guilty of unwarranted exaggeration. On the other, I'm hard-pressed to think of a more theologically important, spiritually encouraging, and

eschatologically controversial statement than that of Paul in 2 Corinthians 6:16: "For we are the temple of the living God"!

The starting point for understanding this crucial concept is the
Old Testament narrative in which we find the visible manifestation
of the splendor of God among his people, the *shekinah* of God, his
majestic and radiant glory without which the Israelites would have
been left in the darkness that characterized the Gentile world.

Before Solomon's temple, God revealed his glory in the tent or
tabernacle that Moses constructed. It was there that God would
come, dwell, and meet with his people. "Let them make me a sanctuary," the Lord spoke to Moses, "that I may dwell in their midst" (Ex.
25:8). It was there that "the pillar of cloud would descend and stand
at the entrance of the tent, and [there] the LORD would speak with
Moses" (Ex. 33:9). It was there that "the cloud covered the tent of
meeting, and the glory of the LORD filled the tabernacle" (Ex. 40:34).
The tabernacle was where the people of Israel would draw near to
hear from God, to worship God, and to stand in his presence (see
Lev. 9:23; Num. 14:10).

What was true of the tabernacle during the days of Israel's sojourn
was even more the case in the temple of Solomon. When the ark
of the covenant was brought "to its place, in the inner sanctuary
of the house, in the Most Holy Place, underneath the wings of the
cherubim" (2 Chron. 5:7), "the priests could not stand to minister
because of the cloud, for the glory of the LORD filled the house of
God" (2 Chron. 5:14).

It is against this preparatory backdrop that we read John's stunning declaration that "the Word became flesh and dwelt among us,
and we have seen his glory, glory as of the only Son from the Father,
full of grace and truth" (John 1:14). The word translated "dwelt"
(*skenoo*) literally means "to pitch a tent" or "to live in a tabernacle"
and unmistakably points back to the Old Testament when God's
glory took up residence in the tent of Moses, the portable tabernacle,
and eventually in Solomon's temple.

John's point is that God has now chosen to dwell with his people
in a yet more personal way, in the Word who became flesh: in Jesus!
The Word, Jesus of Nazareth, is the true and ultimate *shekinah* glory
of God, the complete and perfect manifestation of the presence of

God among his people. The place of God's glorious dwelling is the flesh of his Son! The glory that once shined in the tent/tabernacle/temple of old, veiled in the mysterious cloud, was simply *a foreglow, a mere anticipatory flicker*, if you will, of that exceedingly excelling glory now embodied in the incarnate Word, Jesus Christ (see Col. 1:19).

God no longer lives in a tent or tabernacle built by human hands, *nor will he ever*. God's glorious manifest presence is not to be found in an ornate temple of marble, gold, and precious stones, but rather in Jesus. Jesus is the glory of God in human flesh, the one in whom God has finally and fully pitched his tent.

The point is that the temple of the old covenant was a type or foreshadowing of the glory of Christ. It was the place where the Law of Moses was preserved, of which Jesus is now the fulfillment. It was the place of revelation and relationship, where God met and spoke to his people. Now we hear God and see God and meet God in Jesus. It was the place of sacrifice, where forgiveness of sins was obtained. For that, we now go to Jesus. Israel worshiped and celebrated in the temple in Jerusalem. We now worship in spirit and truth, regardless of geographical locale (see John 4:20–26).

To meet God, to talk with God, to worship God, you no longer come to a building or a tent or a structure made with human hands. You come to Jesus! Jesus is the Temple of God!

But the story doesn't end there. *We, the church, are the body of Christ* and therefore constitute the temple in which God is pleased to dwell. The *shekinah* of Yahweh now abides permanently and powerfully in us through the Holy Spirit. When Paul describes this in his letter to the Ephesians, he refers to Jesus Christ as the cornerstone, "in whom the whole structure, being joined together, grows into a holy temple in the Lord. In him you also are being built together into a dwelling place for God by the Spirit" (Eph. 2:21–22). Simply put, God's residence is "neither a literal temple in Jerusalem nor simply heaven, but the Church, of which the Gentile Christian readers in Asia Minor were a part."[1]

This formation of the temple is an ongoing divine project, a continuous process (see also Eph. 4:15–16). Although it may seem strange to speak of a "building" experiencing continuous "growth,"

Paul surely wants us to conceive of the church as an *organic* entity. Recall that Peter also refers to believers somewhat paradoxically as "living stones" (1 Pet. 2:5)!

Again, Paul grounds his appeal to the Corinthians in this truth: "Do you not know that *you are God's temple* and that God's Spirit dwells in you? If anyone destroys God's temple, God will destroy him. For God's temple is holy, and you are that temple" (1 Cor. 3:16–17). In his plea for sexual purity, he again asks: "Or do you not know that *your body is a temple of the Holy Spirit within you,* whom you have from God? You are not your own, for you were bought with a price. So glorify God in your body" (1 Cor. 6:19–20; see also the graphic portrayal of this truth in 1 Pet. 2:4–10).

All this bring us to Paul's consummate declaration in 2 Corinthians 6:16: "For we are the temple of the living God"! To reinforce this point he conflates several Old Testament texts (Lev. 26:11–12; Isa. 52:11; Ezek. 11:17; 20:34, 41) that prophesied of a coming, end-times temple, one of which is described in Ezekiel 37:26–27 where God declares: "I will make a covenant of peace with them. It shall be an everlasting covenant with them. And I will set them in their land and multiply them, and will set my sanctuary in their midst forevermore. My dwelling place shall be with them, and I will be their God, and they shall be my people."

Let me come to the point: Beginning with the incarnation and consummating in the resurrection of Jesus Christ, together with the progressive building of his spiritual body, the church, God is fulfilling his promise of an eschatological temple in which he will forever dwell.

But what of the literal, physical temple in Jerusalem? Has it lost its spiritual significance in God's redemptive purposes? To answer this we must return to Jesus' words in Matthew 23–24.

In judgment against the Jewish people, our Lord abandoned the temple complex, both physically and spiritually, as he departed and made his way to the Mount of Olives. "Your house," Jesus said, "is left to you desolate" (Matt. 23:38). It has thus ceased to be "God's" house. When Jesus died and "the curtain of the temple was torn in two, from top to bottom" (Matt. 27:51), God forever ceased to bless

227

it with his presence or to acknowledge it as anything other than *ichabod* (the glory has departed).

Just as dramatically as Jesus had entered Jerusalem (Matt. 21:1–17, the so-called "Triumphal Entry") and its temple, he now departs. This once grand and glorious house of God is now consigned exclusively to the Jewish people and their religious leaders ("See, *your* house is left to *you* desolate," Matt. 23:38). The echoes of God's withdrawal from the temple in Ezekiel's vision reverberate in the words of our Lord (see Ezek. 10:18–19; 11:22–23). The ultimate physical destruction of the temple by the Romans in AD 70 is but the outward consummation of God's spiritual repudiation of it. Jesus has now left, never to return. Indeed, the action of Jesus in departing the temple and taking his seat on the Mount of Olives (Matt. 24:3) recalls Ezekiel 11:23 where we read that "the glory of the LORD went up from the midst of the city and stood on the mountain that is on the east side of the city."

This applies equally to any supposed future temple that many believe will be built in Jerusalem in the general vicinity where the Dome of the Rock now stands. It's entirely possible, of course, that people in Israel may one day build a temple structure and resume their religious activities within it. The political and military implications of such, not to mention the religious furor it would provoke, are obvious.

Whether or not this will ever occur is hard to say, but if it does it will have no eschatological or theological significance whatsoever, other than to rise up as a stench in the nostrils of God. The only temple in which God is now and forever will be pleased to dwell is Jesus Christ and the church, his spiritual body.

It would be an egregious expression of the worst imaginable *redemptive regression* to suggest that God would ever sanction the rebuilding of the temple. It would be tantamount to a denial that the Word became flesh and dwelt among us. It would constitute a repudiation of the church as the temple of God and thus an affront to the explicit affirmation of Paul here in 2 Corinthians 6 and elsewhere.

Finally, let's not lose sight of the practical point Paul is making. It is because we as the church are the place of God's presence in the world today that we must guard ourselves against any and every expression of idolatry. We are not simply another cultural institution or "social service meeting the felt needs" of our neighbors. "Instead, as the new covenant people of God, the church is the 'family of God' united by a common identity in Christ and gathered around her common worship and fear of 'the Lord Almighty.'"[2] May our lives always reflect that glorious and gracious identity.

Notes

Introduction to 2 Corinthians

1. Corinth was eventually destroyed by an earthquake in AD 521, never to be rebuilt.

2. D. A. Carson, Douglas J. Moo, and Leon Morris, *An Introduction to the New Testament* (Grand Rapids: Zondervan, 1992), 263.

3. Gordon D. Fee, *The First Epistle to the Corinthians* (Grand Rapids: Eerdmans, 1987), 4.

4. The following commentaries have greatly helped me reconstruct these events: D. A. Carson, *From Triumphalism to Maturity: An Exposition of 2 Corinthians 10–13* (Grand Rapids: Baker, 1984); Philip E. Hughes, *Paul's Second Epistle to the Corinthians* (Grand Rapids: Eerdmans, 1973); Paul Barnett, *The Second Epistle to the Corinthians* (Grand Rapids: Eerdmans, 1997); Ralph P. Martin, *2 Corinthians*, Word Biblical Commentary (Waco: Word Books, 1986); and Murray J. Harris, *The Second Epistle to the Corinthians: A Commentary on the Greek Text* (Grand Rapids: Eerdmans, 2005).

5. Barnett, *Second Epistle to the Corinthians*, 14.

6. If you are unsure of how to respond to the idea of apostolic letters that were not preserved and thus did not make their way into the biblical canon, I encourage you to read my explanation *The Hope of Glory: 100 Daily Meditations in Colossians* (Wheaton, IL: Crossway, 2008), 351–54.

7. The most extensive defense of this view is found in the commentary by Victor Furnish, *II Corinthians*, The Anchor Bible (Garden City: Doubleday, 1984), a response to which is found in Barnett, *Second Epistle to the Corinthians*, 17. See also the extensive response found in Carson, Moo, Morris, *Introduction to the New Testament*, 268–71.

8. D. A. Carson, *From Triumphalism to Maturity*, 14.

Chapter 1: Father of Mercies, God of All Comfort

1. Murray J. Harris, *The Second Epistle to the Corinthians: A Commentary on the Greek Text* (Grand Rapids: Eerdmans, 2005), 142–43.

Chapter 2: Conduits of Divine Comfort

1. Murray J. Harris, *The Second Epistle to the Corinthians: A Commentary on the Greek Text* (Grand Rapids: Eerdmans, 2005), 144.

2. James Denney, *The Second Epistle to the Corinthians* (London: Hodder and Stoughton, 1894), 18.

3. Paul Barnett, *The Second Epistle to the Corinthians* (Grand Rapids: Eerdmans, 1997), 73.

4. Ibid., 77.

5. Harris, *Second Epistle to the Corinthians*, 149.

Chapter 3: God's Design in Our Distress

1. Murray J. Harris, *The Second Epistle to the Corinthians: A Commentary on the Greek Text* (Grand Rapids: Eerdmans, 2005), 154.

2. Ibid., 156.

3. James Denney, *The Second Epistle to the Corinthians* (London: Hodder and Stoughton, 1894), 24–25 (emphasis added).

Chapter 4: Prayer: Dealing with Our Doubts

1. Gordon P. Wiles, *Paul's Intercessory Prayers: The Significance of the Intercessory Prayer Passages in the Letters of St. Paul* (London: Cambridge University Press, 1974), 269.

Chapter 5: When Christians Misunderstand Christians

1. James Denney, *The Second Epistle to the Corinthians* (London: Hodder and Stoughton, 1894), 37–38.

Chapter 6: It Was Grace That Did It

1. Scott Hafemann, *2 Corinthians*, NIV Application Commentary (Grand Rapids: Zondervan, 2000), 82.

2. Murray J. Harris, *The Second Epistle to the Corinthians: A Commentary on the Greek Text* (Grand Rapids: Eerdmans, 2005), 185.

Chapter 8: Cinderella No More

1. Alister E. McGrath, *Christian Theology: An Introduction* (Oxford, UK: Blackwell, 1994), 240.

2. Gordon Fee, *God's Empowering Presence: The Holy Spirit in the Letters of Paul* (Peabody, MA: Hendrickson, 1994), 807.

3. Ibid.

4. John Eadie, *A Commentary on the Greek Text of the Epistle of Paul to the Ephesians* (Grand Rapids: Kregel, 1861), 67–68.

5. Peter T. O'Brien, *The Letter to the Ephesians* (Grand Rapids: Eerdmans, 1999), 121.

Chapter 10: Reflections on Church Discipline

1. Paul Barnett, *The Second Epistle to the Corinthians* (Grand Rapids: Eerdmans, 1997), 124.

2. Philip E. Hughes, *Paul's Second Epistle to the Corinthians* (Grand Rapids: Eerdmans, 1973), 66–67.

Chapter 11: Satanic Stratagems

1. Sydney Page, *Powers of Evil: A Biblical Study of Satan and Demons* (Grand Rapids: Baker, 1995), 132.

2. Ibid., 124.

Chapter 12: The Dangers of Triumphalism

1. John Calvin, *The Second Epistle of Paul the Apostle to the Corinthians*, trans. T. A. Smail (Grand Rapids: Eerdmans, 1973), 33.

2. C. K. Barrett, *A Commentary on the Second Epistle to the Corinthians* (New York: Harper & Row, 1973), 95–105.

3. Paul Barnett, *The Second Epistle to the Corinthians* (Grand Rapids: Eerdmans, 1997), 150.

4. Ibid., 152.

5. Ben Witherington III, *Conflict and Community in Corinth: A Socio-Rhetorical Commentary on 1 and 2 Corinthians* (Grand Rapids: Eerdmans, 1995), 366.

Chapter 14: Is Anyone Sufficient for These Things? Yes!

1. Scott J. Hafemann, *2 Corinthians*, NIV Application Commentary (Grand Rapids: Zondervan, 2000), 113.

2. Murray J. Harris, *The Second Epistle to the Corinthians: A Commentary on the Greek Text* (Grand Rapids: Eerdmans, 2005), 253.

3. Hafemann, *2 Corinthians*, 114–15.

Chapter 15: Epistles of Christ

1. Scott Hafemann, *2 Corinthians*, NIV Application Commentary (Grand Rapids: Zondervan, 2000), 116.

2. Paul Barnett, *The Second Epistle to the Corinthians* (Grand Rapids: Eerdmans, 1997), 166.

3. Hafemann, *2 Corinthians*, 122–23.

4. Ibid., 123.

Chapter 16: The Surpassing Glory of the New Covenant

1. Scott Hafemann, *2 Corinthians*, NIV Application Commentary (Grand Rapids: Zondervan, 2000), 132.

Chapter 17: Bumped along the Pathway to Glory

1. Murray J. Harris, *The Second Epistle to the Corinthians: A Commentary on the Greek Text* (Grand Rapids: Eerdmans, 2005), 317.

2. Paul Barnett, *The Second Epistle to the Corinthians* (Grand Rapids: Eerdmans, 1997), 206.

3. Gordon Fee, *God's Empowering Presence: The Holy Spirit in the Letters of Paul* (Peabody, MA: Hendrickson, 1994), 317.

4. Harris, *Second Epistle to the Corinthians*, 316.

5. John Piper, *The Pleasures of God* (Portland, OR: Multnomah, 1991), 17.

Chapter 18: Fighting Discouragement

1. Murray J. Harris, *The Second Epistle to the Corinthians: A Commentary on the Greek Text* (Grand Rapids: Eerdmans, 2005), 323.

Chapter 19: Tampering with God's Word

1. Complementarianism is the belief that whereas men and women equally bear the image of God, they also are assigned differing, though complementary, roles and responsibilities in the church and home.

2. See George Barna, *Revolution* (Wheaton, IL: Tyndale, 2005).

3. *Leadership*, Fall 2007, 19–20.

Chapter 20: The Gospel: Veiled and Unveiled

1. John R. W. Stott, *The Letters of John* (Grand Rapids: Eerdmans, 1996), 196.

2. John Calvin, *The Second Epistle of Paul the Apostle to the Corinthians*, trans. T. A. Smail (Grand Rapids: Eerdmans, 1973), 53.

3. Scott Hafemann, *2 Corinthians*, NIV Application Commentary (Grand Rapids: Zondervan, 2000), 177.

Chapter 21: A Divine and Supernatural Light

1. John Piper, "A Divine and Supernatural Light Immediately Imparted to the Soul by the Spirit of God: An Edwardsean Sermon (2 Corinthians 3:18–4:7)," in *A God Entranced Vision of All Things*, ed. John Piper and Justin Taylor (Wheaton, IL: Crossway Books, 2004), 259.

2. Paul Barnett, *The Second Epistle to the Corinthians* (Grand Rapids: Eerdmans, 1997), 219–20.

3. Jonathan Edwards, "A Divine and Supernatural Light," in *A Jonathan Edwards Reader*, ed. John E. Smith, Harry S. Stout, and Kenneth P. Minkema (New Haven, CT: Yale University Press, 1995), 110.

4. Ibid., 111.

5. Ibid.

6. Ibid., 112.

7. Ibid. Emphasis added.

8. Ibid.

9. Ibid., 123.

Chapter 22: Jars of Clay and the Glory of God

1. Philip E. Hughes, *Paul's Second Epistle to the Corinthians* (Grand Rapids: Eerdmans, 1973), 135.

2. Ibid., 137. See also 1 Corinthians 1:26–29.

Chapter 23: Knocked Down, but Not Out

1. Philip E. Hughes, *Paul's Second Epistle to the Corinthians* (Grand Rapids: Eerdmans, 1973), 138–39.

2. Murray J. Harris, *The Second Epistle to the Corinthians: A Commentary on the Greek Text* (Grand Rapids: Eerdmans, 2005), 342.

3. C. K. Barrett, *A Commentary on the Second Epistle to the Corinthians* (New York: Harper & Row, 1973), 136.

4. Hughes, *Paul's Second Epistle*, 138.

5. Paul Barnett, *The Second Epistle to the Corinthians* (Grand Rapids: Eerdmans, 1997), 236.

6. Harris, *Second Epistle to the Corinthians*, 347.

7. Scott Hafemann, *2 Corinthians*, NIV Application Commentary (Grand Rapids: Zondervan, 2000), 184.

Chapter 25: Gazing Intently at What You Can't See

1. R. C. H. Lenski, *The Interpretation of St. Paul's First and Second Epistles to the Corinthians* (Minneapolis: Augsburg, 1963).

2. Murray J. Harris, *The Second Epistle to the Corinthians: A Commentary on the Greek Text* (Grand Rapids: Eerdmans, 2005), 363.

3. Philip E. Hughes, *Paul's Second Epistle to the Corinthians* (Grand Rapids: Eerdmans, 1973), 157–58.

4. Paul Barnett, *The Second Epistle to the Corinthians* (Grand Rapids: Eerdmans, 1997), 252–53.

Chapter 26: What Happens When a Christian Dies? (1)

1. Philip E. Hughes, *Paul's Second Epistle to the Corinthians* (Grand Rapids: Eerdmans, 1973), 174.

Chapter 27: What Happens When a Christian Dies? (2)

1. John Calvin, *Institutes of the Christian Religion*, ed. John T. McNeill, trans. Ford Lewis Battles (Philadelphia: Westminster Press, 1975), 3.9.5.

2. Murray J. Harris, *The Second Epistle to the Corinthians: A Commentary on the Greek Text* (Grand Rapids: Eerdmans, 2005), 397–98.

3. Ibid., 402 (emphasis added).

4. Adolphe Monod, *Adolphe Monod's Farewell to His Friends and to His Church*, trans. Owen Thomas (London: Banner of Truth, 1962), 11.

5. For more on this, go to my Web site, www.samstorms.com and click on Theological Studies, then Roman Catholicism, then Purgatory.

Chapter 28: What Happens When a Christian Dies? (3)

1. Murray J. Harris, *The Second Epistle to the Corinthians: A Commentary on the Greek Text* (Grand Rapids: Eerdmans, 2005), 406.

2. Ibid., 405.

3. Ibid., 406.

4. Sam Storms, *One Thing: Developing a Passion for the Beauty of God* (Fearn, Ross-shire, Scotland: Christian Focus, 2004), 180–81.

Chapter 29: You, Others, and the Judgment Seat of Christ

1. Scott Hafemann, *2 Corinthians*, NIV Application Commentary (Grand Rapids: Zondervan, 2000), 238.

Chapter 30: "Out of His Mind" for God

1. Murray J. Harris, *The Second Epistle to the Corinthians: A Commentary on the Greek Text* (Grand Rapids: Eerdmans, 2005), 417.

2. Ralph P. Martin, *2 Corinthians*, Word Biblical Commentary (Waco, TX: Word, 1986), 127.

Chapter 31: The Controlling Power of the Cross

1. James Denney, *The Second Epistle to the Corinthians* (London: Hodder and Stoughton, 1894), 194–95.

Chapter 33: Seeing Others Spiritually: A Practical Consequence of the Cross

1. Scott Hafemann, *2 Corinthians*, NIV Application Commentary (Grand Rapids: Zondervan, 2000), 242.

2. Murray J. Harris, *The Second Epistle to the Corinthians: A Commentary on the Greek Text* (Grand Rapids: Eerdmans, 2005), 429 (cf. Acts 22:3–4; 26:9–11).

Chapter 35: When God Saves Sinners from God

1. James Denney, *The Second Epistle to the Corinthians* (London: Hodder and Stoughton, 1894), 212.

2. Philip E. Hughes, *Paul's Second Epistle to the Corinthians* (Grand Rapids: Eerdmans, 1973), 212.

3. Denney, *Second Epistle to the Corinthians*, 213–15.

Chapter 36: Could Jesus Have Sinned?

1. See www.samstorms.com, "Kenotic View" in Christology, Theological Studies.

2. Gerald F. Hawthorne, *The Presence and the Power* (Dallas: Word, 1991), 208.

3. Ibid., 210.

4. Ibid., 139.

5. Ibid., 234.

Chapter 37: Receiving the Grace of God in Vain

1. Murray J. Harris, *The Second Epistle to the Corinthians: A Commentary on the Greek Text* (Grand Rapids: Eerdmans, 2005), 458.

2. Philip E. Hughes, *Paul's Second Epistle to the Corinthians* (Grand Rapids: Eerdmans, 1973), 218–19.

3. Judith M. Gundry Volf, *Paul and Perseverance: Staying In and Falling Away* (Louisville: Westminster/John Knox Press, 1990), 280.

4. Harris, *Second Epistle to the Corinthians*, 458–59.

5. Ibid., 459.

6. Ibid.

7. Ibid.

Chapter 38: The Most Eloquent Advertisement for the Gospel

1. Murray J. Harris, *The Second Epistle to the Corinthians: A Commentary on the Greek Text* (Grand Rapids: Eerdmans, 2005), 469 (emphasis added).

2. Ibid. Emphasis added.

Chapter 42: What's a Christian to Do?

1. Murray J. Harris, *The Second Epistle to the Corinthians: A Commentary on the Greek Text* (Grand Rapids: Eerdmans, 2005), 474.

Chapter 43: The Treasure, Quite Simply, Is Christ

1. Quoted in Iain Murray, *Jonathan Edwards: A New Biography* (Carlisle, PA: Banner of Truth, 1987), 327.

Chapter 44: Spiritual Schizophrenia

1. Dictionary.com, s.v. "Schizophrenia," www.dictionary.com.

Chapter 45: Dealing with Dysfunction in the Family of Faith

1. Murray J. Harris, *The Second Epistle to the Corinthians: A Commentary on the Greek Text* (Grand Rapids: Eerdmans, 2005), 490.

Chapter 46: The Life of the Church in the World versus the Life of the World in the Church

1. Philip E. Hughes, *Paul's Second Epistle to the Corinthians* (Grand Rapids: Eerdmans, 1973), 251.

2. John Calvin, *The Second Epistle of Paul the Apostle to the Corinthians*, trans. T. A. Smail (Grand Rapids: Eerdmans, 1973), 90.

3. Scott Hafemann, *2 Corinthians*, NIV Application Commentary (Grand Rapids: Zondervan, 2000), 292.

Chapter 47: We Are the Temple of the Living God

1. Andrew T. Lincoln, *Ephesians*, Word Biblical Commentary (Dallas: Word Books, 1990), 158.

2. Scott Hafemann, *2 Corinthians*, NIV Application Commentary (Grand Rapids: Zondervan, 2000), 292.

CPSIA information can be obtained
at www.ICGtesting.com
Printed in the USA
LVHW041510180122
708821LV00006B/252

9 781433 511509